MRS GASKELL & ME

Nell Stevens lives in London where she teaches Creative Writing at Goldsmiths, University of London. She has a Ph.D. in Victorian Literature from King's College London, and an MFA in Fiction from Boston University. She is the author of *Bleaker House* and *Mrs Gaskell & Me*.

Also by Nell Stevens

Bleaker House

Nell Stevens

MRS GASKELL AND ME

Two Women, Two Love Stories,
Two Centuries Apart

PICADOR

First published 2018 by Picador

First published in paperback 2019 by Picador
an imprint of Pan Macmillan
20 New Wharf Road, London N1 9RR
Associated companies throughout the world
www.panmacmillan.com

ISBN 978-1-5098-6821-6

Copyright © Nell Stevens 2018

The right of Nell Stevens to be identified as the
author of this work has been asserted by her in accordance
with the Copyright, Designs and Patents Act 1988.

Permissions Acknowledgements
An extract from 'Something Amazing Just Happened' by Ted Berrigan appears here with
permission from University of California Press Books; Ted Berrigan, *The Selected Poems of Ted
Berrigan*, University of California Press Books, 2011. Gail Mazur, 'Michelangelo: To Giovanni
Da Pistoia When the Author Was Painting the Vault of the Sistine Chapel (by Michelangelo
Buonarroti)' from *Zeppo's First Wife*. Copyright © 2005 by Gail Mazur. Reprinted by permission
of The University of Chicago Press. Source: *They Can't Take That Away from Me* (The University
of Chicago Press, 2001). An extract from 'Poet's Work' by Lorine Niedecker appears here
with permission from University of California Press Books; *Lorine Niedecker: Collected Works*,
University of California Press Books, 2004. Poems by William Story are reproduced courtesy of
the Harry Ransom Center, The University of Texas at Austin. 'The Nineteenth Century and
After' by W. B. Yeats appears in its entirety on page 131. Grateful acknowledgement is made to
United Agents on behalf of Caitríona Yeats.

All rights reserved. No part of this publication may be reproduced,
stored in a retrieval system, or transmitted, in any form, or by any means
(electronic, mechanical, photocopying, recording or otherwise)
without the prior written permission of the publisher.

Pan Macmillan does not have any control over, or any responsibility for,
any author or third-party websites referred to in or on this book.

1 3 5 7 9 8 6 4 2

A CIP catalogue record for this book is available from the British Library.

Printed and bound by CPI Group (UK) Ltd, Croydon, CR0 4YY

This book is sold subject to the condition that it shall not, by way of
trade or otherwise, be lent, hired out, or otherwise circulated without
the publisher's prior consent in any form of binding or cover other than
that in which it is published and without a similar condition including
this condition being imposed on the subsequent purchaser.

Visit **www.picador.com** to read more about all our books
and to buy them. You will also find features, author interviews and
news of any author events, and you can sign up for e-newsletters
so that you're always first to hear about our new releases.

For Amanda, Grace & Claudia

Of writing many books there is no end;
And I who have written much in prose and verse
For others' uses, will write now for mine,-
Will write my story for my better self,
As when you paint your portrait for a friend,
Who keeps it in a drawer and looks at it
Long after he has ceased to love you, just
To hold together what he was and is.

— Elizabeth Barrett Browning

Disclaimer

"Do you mind the law of libel?" Mrs Gaskell wrote to her publisher, when she was working on her biography of Charlotte Brontë in 1856. "I have three people I want to libel."

I have no people I want to libel. I have changed names, scenes, details, motivations and personalities. Every word has been filtered through the distortions of my memory, bias and efforts to tell a story. This is as true of the historical material as it is of the sections about my own life: studies, letters and texts excerpted here are not always faithfully quoted. This is a work of imagination.

Two separate parties threatened legal action against Mrs Gaskell when *The Life of Charlotte Brontë* came out in 1857. I want to be like her in many ways, but not that one.

Part One

BODY STUDY

1855

What You Had

1. A husband

When you wanted to talk about your husband, you talked about sermons. Sermons, you said, bored you. You sometimes called yourself a 'sermon-hater'. In the front row of the Cross Street Chapel, you'd fidget, your mind would wander, as your husband, the minister, preached. You mused about the people in the pews around you – about their lives and secrets, the things that they were thinking about instead of listening to your husband – and when you came back to yourself you found you had missed almost nothing, he was still speaking, the congregation was still waiting in silence, coughing and sighing, crossing and uncrossing their legs.

Sermons, of course, were meant for good; were meant to help you, support you, reform you. And yet, all the same, they were dull, dull, dull, and what you really wanted was to feel something, do something: to be moved, to move, to love.

Your husband: the minister, Mr Gaskell. Sequestered in his study in the middle of your house, in the middle of newly industrial Manchester, square in the middle of the nineteenth century, he was good to the core. He cautioned you when you were reckless or impulsive. He corrected the grammar of your letters before you sent them. He helped you, supported you, reformed you.

And you, Mrs Gaskell, waited outside his study door; you raised a hand to knock, to see if today he would come to the parlour and sit with you and the girls. You wondered whether today, perhaps, you might find in your husband a conversation rather than a sermon. A faint tap, quiet enough that he could pretend, if he wanted, not to hear. You pressed your ear to the wood and listened until it was clear there would be no reply, and then you stood there far longer than you needed to, resting your cheek against the cool surface.

You were always lucky, Mrs Gaskell; you were always grateful for what you had, and yet, all the same, you were restless.

2. A career

Sometimes days on end went by in a blur of what you called Home Life – meals and clothes and correspondence, hosting and visiting – and by the end of it you were tired and grumpy, but not tired in the way you wanted to be. You lay awake, exhausted, your mind alert. Beside you your sleeping husband was eerily still. His body, his very breathing, was moderate, controlled. You imagined moving away, back to the village where you lived as a child, or even somewhere entirely foreign, where nobody knew you, and you could say you were unmarried and had no responsibilities.

4

You told stories all the time, to friends, to yourself; you exaggerated in letters, made up white lies that entertained you and seemed to entertain others too; you gossiped unapologetically. None of this was enough. There were stories left over. Lying awake in the night beside the motionless Mr Gaskell, they overwhelmed you, and yet, you craved them.

You began to keep a diary. It was about the children, you said, to people who asked: a record of their development. But it was about you too – you couldn't keep yourself and your stories out of it – and soon you moved on to articles about culture and country life, and sent them, sheepishly, to magazines. They appeared in print. Next, you published short fiction using a pseudonym: quiet, sad tales about ordinary people like the ones in church, about whose private lives you couldn't help but wonder. And then you wrote a novel called *Mary Barton*, a great big pounding book about the people around you in the city, the ones you saw crammed into factories and warehouses and tenements, whose griefs you could only, and did, imagine. It became the sort of book that people bought and reviewed and talked about, and all of a sudden you had a career.

This thing you had now, this career, was all your own. It was a portal. It drew you away from Manchester, away from Mr Gaskell, to new places and new acquaintances: painters, philosophers, critics. You became friends with Florence Nightingale. You became friends with Charlotte Brontë. At a party in London you met Charles Dickens, who complimented you on *Mary Barton* and you thought, for the rest of the night, over and over: *Charles Dickens has read my book. Charles Dickens has read my book. Charles Dickens.* You paid no attention to the earnest, impressed men and women who spoke to you after that. Your mind was fully occupied: *Charles Dickens has read my book.*

You went home. You wrote more books.

3. A letter

By the time you opened it, the letter was four days old. You had been in Paris and were still giddy from the memory of it. There had been parties in your honour at the house of Madame Mohl, and there had been cream cakes (never enough, but still) and best of all there had been Americans everywhere, intriguing and exotic. You had talked and talked and name-dropped more than you knew you should, and in particular you had boasted of how, thanks to you, your cherished friend Charlotte Brontë was happily married and soon to be a mother. Dear Charlotte: you had encouraged and cajoled her towards accepting the proposal of a smart, earnest curate called Mr Nicholls; she had been reluctant; her father had disapproved; you had known better and helped her see that after all the hardship and grief of her life, a drop of domesticity was exactly what was needed. You had not, then, observed any conflict between your personal feelings about Mr Gaskell, and your advice to Charlotte regarding Mr Nicholls.

In Paris, people had listened to you. People had praised

you. They had given you cake and sherry. In Paris, there had been all your favourite things at once.

At home, the letter was waiting for you, halfway down a stack of correspondence that had amassed from your weeks away. You worked your way down the pile, scanning for gossip. A girl you had known as a child was having marital problems after running up extravagant debts. A prominent writer was entangled in controversy over whether he was the true author of his works. The daughter of a distant cousin was turning twenty-one and considered pretty, would soon be engaged. And then, there it was: a note to say that your friend, Charlotte Brontë, was dead.

4. A project

In place of a friend: a book. You began to think of writing *The Life of Charlotte Brontë* almost at once; it was an outlet for the sharp energy of your grief, and a distraction. You fired off letters to her father, her husband, her publisher, requesting every detail of her life and death, hoping, perhaps, to be asked to write a biography. And eventually the request came from old Mr Brontë: *Finding that a great many scribblers, as well as some clever and truthful writers, have published articles, in Newspapers, and tracts – respecting my Dear Daughter Charlotte, since her death – and seeing that many things that have been stated, are true, but more false* . . . He wanted an official biography to set the record straight. *You seem to me to be the best qualified for doing what I wish should be done*, he said. *Could my Daughter speak from the tomb, I feel certain, she would laud our choice.*

Mrs Gaskell: at the ready. Mrs Gaskell: pen aloft and in possession of a new project.

You had always loved ghost stories, after all, and Charlotte, even in life, was nothing if not ghostly. She had paced between the corners of her dim little parlour, muttering to herself after dark. Her siblings, one after the other, had slid before her into the grave: Maria, Elizabeth, Branwell, Emily, Anne. And the deathly expanses of the moors stretching away from the parsonage in Haworth: you had walked them with her, and felt for yourself the chill of the fog, the suck of the boggy ground underfoot. It was a real-life ghost story waiting to be told, waiting for you to tell it. *The Life of Charlotte Brontë* would practically write itself.

But Charlotte had been brash, too, and usually at the wrong times. She had written big and tricky books that made faraway readers in London raise their eyebrows. There was a whiff of sex and lust and impulsiveness about Charlotte and her stories. She was not, exactly, proper. Ghostly, yes, but also, often, a little too alive.

For this you had never judged her. People wrote outraged nonsense about your books, too. You knew what it was to be a woman with a career, to be a woman who wrote about everything in life, even the unpleasant things. You knew, too, the use of a husband, of children, to persuade your critics that while your books might be wild and alarming, you yourself were well-mannered, dutiful and tame. And so you had clucked and mothered her, as

8

you did everyone, and for her protection and her happiness you had done your best to drag her onto the terra firma of domestic life. Despite your personal antipathy to sermons, you had thought that marriage to Mr Nicholls the Curate would make Charlotte happy. You really had.

You had encouraged her to marry, to keep her safe: irony of ironies that her pregnancy killed her. Did you begin, at once, to blame yourself? Was the project of writing her biography doomed from the start by your own uneasy conscience?

The Life of Charlotte Brontë took two years to write and more pain and worry than you could possibly have anticipated. There were so many people to insult: the terrible master of the school that caused the deaths of two of the Brontë girls, and which Charlotte described in the opening chapters of *Jane Eyre*; the married woman who had seduced and ruined Branwell Brontë; the Belgian teacher after whom Charlotte had pined so openly and so embarrassingly. You sent frantic letters to your publisher enquiring about libel laws. There were so many people, you said, whom you wanted to libel.

And everyone, all the time, was offended. If you suggested the story was one way, someone would write and correct you. If you suggested it differently, someone else complained, would swamp your desk with letters detailing the true facts of the matter. You owed it to your dead friend to tell the truth, but the truth was evasive and slippery and fought back tooth and nail from the page.

Mr Gaskell's sermons were unwavering on the subject. They made honesty sound so simple. How easy it was, they implied, to live honestly. But you were not Mr Gaskell. You were not a minister. You were a writer, and to you, everything was complicated.

5. A plan

The Life of Charlotte Brontë was no fun to write, and everybody was angry about it, even before it was published, and you found that when you did manage to fall asleep you'd wake, heart racing and sweat prickling along your breastbone. Your mind was full of new, competing visions of how it might all go wrong, how your attempt to write a book about your friend might end with the disgrace not only of you and your family but of her and hers.

Your nerves were overactive, but perceptive, too. You must have seen the trouble coming, because, amid the chaos of writing and letters from your publisher and letters from Mr Brontë, the general noise of Manchester life and the sermons, the demands of daughters and friends, the idea came to you that when the work was done and the book was finally out in the world, you would escape the reviews and go, instead, to Rome.

2013

Eurostar

There is a sniffer on the 4 p.m. train from London St Pancras to Paris Gare du Nord. From my window seat with a view of the black wall of the Channel Tunnel, I hear it: the rumble and hiss of the wheels on the tracks, the giggles of a child playing peek-a-boo with its mother, the murmur of conversation at the far end of the carriage, and then, sporadically, that loud, wet sniff. I crane my head around to get a look at the culprit: a man in a suit who is frowning at his laptop over an inflamed nose. If he does it again, I decide, I will offer him a tissue, passive-aggressively. But then of course he does do it again, and all I do is glare, which he doesn't notice. I drum my fingers against the tray table in front of me, which must be at least as annoying to people nearby. I jiggle my knee up and down.

I'm on edge. If it wasn't the sniffer driving me crazy, it would be something else.

I am going to Paris to visit my friend Max, who has recently moved to a top-floor apartment in the second *arrondissement*, and with whom I have been pathetically, persistently in love for the past year. We were in the same fiction workshop at Boston University, and at the beginning of the summer, we graduated; I haven't seen him since. It is autumn now, and our cohort has been scattered across the globe: some to New York, some to LA; one girl is teaching English in Turkey, another is in Romania on a research fellowship. I have returned home to London to begin a Ph.D. in nineteenth-century literature; Max has moved to Paris to write.

The London I have left behind is at its loveliest: crisp and leafy, just beginning to turn mulchy, and the drizzle-grey texture of the streets and buildings is delightful to me after a year abroad. Ahead, on the other side of the tunnel: Paris, an apartment in a tall, old building near Les Halles, and inside it, the man I love – the man who has made it abundantly clear on repeated occasions that he does not love me back.

I am on my way to Paris to make a declaration.

Evidence to suggest that Max is not in love with me:

1. When, early on in our year at Boston University, I forwarded an email advertising a poetry reading to him, suggesting we go together, he replied the day after the event, apologizing for 'only having seen this just now'.

2. When I was standing in line to get a coffee at the campus cafe before class, he walked in, saw me, turned around and left.

3. Once, towards the end of the year, he gave me a lift home and as we drew up outside my house I took a deep breath and said, tremblingly, 'I need

to tell you something.' He said, 'What?' and I said, 'I like you,' and he said, 'Well, I like you too,' and patted me on the knee.

4. When, after the knee-patting incident, I worried that the phrase 'I like you' was open to too broad a spectrum of interpretation and followed up with an email saying, 'Just to clarify, what I was trying to say is that I have had feelings for you all year,' there was a long silence, and then, eventually, he suggested, in a one-line message, that we meet for dinner the next day at a place called Lineage in Coolidge Corner. At the restaurant, we talked about everything we could think of except my email. We got through starters, mains, dessert, coffee: no mention. Afterwards, we went out into torrential rain, and he lent me his coat and we linked arms and walked, bent over, through the downpour to his car. I could feel the heat of him pressing against me, and by the time we reached the parking lot we were both completely drenched and my cheap, worn-out shoes were disintegrating around my feet, and instead of getting into the car he stood by it and looked at me and I thought, *This is it. He's going to kiss me now*, and I waited and the rain thudded onto our faces and then he turned and opened the passenger-side door. I hesitated, and then got in. Max dashed round and ducked into the driver's seat, but, once there, he didn't start the engine, just sat and stared at his hands on the steering wheel for a very long time.

'I'm not looking for a relationship right now,' he said. And then he drove me home.

Somehow, after the incident in the car park, Max and I salvaged a friendship. We spent our final weeks in Boston working on a pilot script for a TV show about a nine-teenth-century music-hall performer loosely based on the life of a real musician called George Leybourne. The script entertained us endlessly, and we spent hours composing lyrics to music-hall songs. It was an easy distraction from the awkwardness of our previous encounters. We went out for dinner at Lineage a lot, and to see films at the Coolidge Corner Theatre, and often we would text each other last thing and first thing: goodnight, good morn-ing. We were, in the disapproving words of my friend Holly, 'dry dating', and it was fun – so much fun that for a while I wondered whether this was, after all, enough. He never once mentioned the knee-patting, the email, and whenever I, towards the end of an evening spent sharing a bottle of wine, looked as though I might be about to bring it up, he steered the conversation away from it so expertly that I lost momentum and forgot what I had been about to say.

I was persuaded by Max's tact: why should the fact that I was in love with him stop us being friends? Why shouldn't I have dinner with this beautiful, well-dressed former lawyer who gave up his job to become a writer and made me laugh and drove me home and loved all the same books as me, and who wrote quiet, immaculate short stories about sad bachelors that were always a perfect balance of hilarious and gut-wrenching?

Except that now I lived in London and he lived in Paris and I was beginning my Ph.D. and he was writing in cafes and wandering by the Seine and life, in short, had moved on. Being in love with Max was all well and good, but it did seem to preclude being in love with anyone else – someone who might, if I was lucky, actually love me back – and so, when Max invited me to stay with him in Paris for a few days, I accepted, but I told myself it was time to make the declaration.

I can't be your friend any more, I was going to say. *I have to fall out of love with you, and if I'm going to do that, I can't be your friend.*

I would spend the weekend with Max; we would go to the Louvre and the Eiffel Tower and climb up the steps to the Sacré-Cœur and it would be lovely, but it would also, though he wouldn't know it at first, be a goodbye. At some point before I left, I'd explain why I could never see him again, and it would be sickening and I would probably feel numb and empty and horribly lonely for weeks, but it was necessary. At some point in the future I would wake up in London and realize that I was all right again. I would be ready to start afresh.

The train slows as it reaches Paris, sliding past the grey tower blocks of the *banlieu*, between banks of graffiti. The sky above the buildings is soft and dense. The sniffer sniffs again, and the peek-a-boo child begins jumping up and down, shouting, 'On est là! On est là!' and as I stand to take down my case from the luggage rack I feel unsteady on my feet, and wish the journey could go on longer. The glass roof of the Gare du Nord extends over the carriage like a grasping hand. The train crawls on, and then stops.

Air outside: crisp. Sound of the station: echoey and deep behind the clatter and rumbling of suitcase wheels. The sniffer: vanished into the crowd. My heart: nervously arrhythmic. At the end of the platform, behind a barrier, surrounded by the expectant smiles of people waiting for other passengers from the London train: Max's face.

1857

Manchester to Rome

Manchester to Dover, Dover to Calais, Calais to Paris. Three nights at the Hôtel des Missions Étrangères on the Rue du Bac (drizzly, chilly) and then onwards. Train pulling out of the Paris station. Chatter of your daughters. Thrum of the wheels on the just-opened railway line, everything newly painted, gleaming, bright: the furthest south that you had ever been. Dijon. Lyon. Avignon. Marseille: another overnight stay – Hôtel de l'Orient on the Rue Grignon, wide shuttered windows and the street outside lit up in the morning with sharp, clear sunshine – and then off again. After six days of travelling, you set sail, at last, for Italy.

'I want just, if I can, to leave England on the day of publication of my book,' you had written to Emelyn Story, your American friend who lived in Rome. And you did exactly that. You were frantic, getting everything in place for your *Life of Charlotte Brontë* to enter the world on time, and when you were certain you could pull it off you wrote again: 'We are really and truly coming to Rome!!!!!!' You would spend three months in the city, leaving Mr Gaskell to his sermons in Manchester, and taking with you your two eldest girls, Marianne, twenty-three, and Meta, twenty.

You hurled your biography of Charlotte into the world like a grenade, and ran away just as fast as you could. You did not look back as you boarded the steam liner at Marseille, to see what chaos you were leaving in your wake.

'Shall we truly see Rome?' you asked Emelyn. 'I don't believe it. It is a dream! I shall never believe it, and shall have to keep pinching myself!'

You stood on the deck of the *Hellespont* and looked forwards at the blue sea, the blue horizon. To your left: the gleaming bulk of the Château d'If, squatting confidently on white rocks.

'Oh, it's just like in *The Count of Monte Cristo*!' said Marianne.

Meta snorted. 'It isn't at all.'

'No,' you said, quietly. 'In the book he calls it a "gloomy fortress" but really it's quite cheerful to look at.'

'It's hardly a "black and frowning rock",' said Meta, gesturing at the white island, which shone as the sun hit it.

'I don't mean *like* in the book,' Marianne said. 'I just mean, it's *in* the book. It's *from* the book.'

'Lock me up there any day,' said Meta. 'It would be like a holiday for ever.'

'It's so pretty,' you said. 'It's so bright.'

Everything was suddenly cheerful. Manchester's grime, the constant smoke and grease of the factories, peeled away from your skin. With each wave the ship broke, the house on Plymouth Grove was further off and felt that way: irrelevant, as though it belonged to someone else, a different Mrs Gaskell. You had many versions of yourself, competing for attention and dominance: wife, mother, philanthropist, gossip, writer. On the ship, you somehow left all of them behind. You were forty-six years old, but devoted to childishness. You were living in a world you had only read about: *The Count of Monte Cristo*, Byron, *Corinne*. You were inside your most precious books, and everything was gleaming.

In Manchester, sunset was a brown tinge behind the brown smoke heaving from the chimneys. On the ocean, now, it was a performance, as though the sky and sea and even the birds conspired to bring you pleasure: you sat with your daughters on deck and gaped at the colours overhead, and the way the water sucked the pinks and oranges down into itself, and how, later, in the darkness, small flowers of phosphorescence bloomed in the waves and moved in strange swirls, like murmurations of starlings, 'like the Milky Way,' Marianne said. In the morning, if you got up early, which you never normally liked to do but seemed to manage at sea, you saw it all again in reverse: the darkness falling away and in its place an optimistic flag of dawn colours.

You were sitting out on deck drinking coffee and gazing at the sky when there was a thud – you felt it in your own stomach – and a shudder that started in the very heart of the ship and continued until you were shaking, too, and Meta was trembling and looked at you wide-eyed and sounded so young, as though she was only ten years old, when she said, 'Mama? What was that?'

People scrambled up from their cabins half-dressed, unsteady. The steerage passengers emerged, too, talking fast in foreign languages, gesturing at something beneath their feet. A woman in only her nightgown, clutching a baby and squinting in the light. Tides of steam rising from below, obscuring everything, and then an eerie stillness as the ship stopped moving. You waited. Suddenly you were aware of the sounds of the waves as they slapped the sides of the ship. The moment of sinking, of being sucked under the water, felt inevitable.

And it was now, in this nauseating pause, that you realized that you truly had believed in Rome, had not only believed but relied on it. You had been miserable in Manchester. Your friend had died. You had done your best to write a book, a good book, and everybody had complained about it, and the one hopeful thing through all of it had been that when it was done you were going to Rome. Were you really going to drown, never having seen the Colosseum?

You were afraid for yourself, but more so for your girls, who were looking at you as though you could, singlehandedly, keep the ship afloat. You reverted to being a mother and clucked at them that everything would be perfectly fine. When the *Hellespont* had retreated safely to Marseilles, its boiler burst but not wrecked, you pretended you had never doubted it.

You did not drown. Instead, you waited for another ship, more seaworthy. You sent a man off to telegraph the Storys and let them know not to panic when the *Helles-pont* failed to arrive. Later, you, your daughters and your luggage were packed onto a little boat that ferried you across the bay to the *Oran*, and as you rearranged yourself in the new cabin and took stock of the day, it was lodged in your heart with a sudden and fierce determination: you were going to Rome if it killed you. Not a dream, not a wish, not a story in a book. Really, truly, Rome.

Stumbling off the ship at Civitavecchia, you tried to detect whether, just by breathing the air, you could tell you were in Italy. There was a tremendous fuss about passports and visas, endless queuing and shuffling of papers, and then you were told you had been waiting in the wrong line and to go to the back of a different one. One of Marianne's boxes was lost and you had to send a boy to find it. Perhaps it was your fate to be interminably delayed. The box reappeared and with it half a dozen boys, none of them the one you had sent, all claiming responsibility for finding it and demanding payment. Then, at last, the passports were stamped, the correct boy rewarded, and you were waved through.

You drove all day towards Rome and grew so tired of looking out for the dome of St Peter's that you dozed and when, suddenly, you saw it, the basilica was up close and looming.

'Look! The Colonnade!'

'The Vatican!'

'St Angelo!'

You knew each monument, each building, from books.

So this was Rome. Inside it, amongst the ruins and monuments and art, were the people with whom you would fall, generally and liberally, in love; and inside it was one person with whom you would fall, specifically, in love.

In the first category there was, at the heart of everything, Mr William Wetmore Story: American sculptor, poet, polymath, who threw wild, wonderful parties and put on plays in his own parlour in which he was the star. He was always busy, always about to execute some new plan that would, he assured you, change the cultural worlds of England and America for ever. He claimed to speak more languages than you knew existed, though you only heard his English, French, Italian and schoolboy Latin. He told stories about the tourists who visited his studio that made you weep with laughter: how precisely he skewered the pretensions of the amateur art critic, how beautifully he acknowledged, with a glint in his eyes and smile, that the subject of the send-up was himself, and you, and all your friends, too. You had asked Mr Story if he and Emelyn would put you up for your first few days in Rome, just until you found your own lodgings, but you had hoped he might offer to have you the whole time. You were not disappointed. The Storys insisted. Their home, Casa Cabrale on the Via Sant'Isidoro, became yours.

Next: funny little Harriet Hosmer, also a sculptor. She

was a squat American, who dressed like a man and rode her horse like a man and refused to notice anyone who was shocked by it. She made statues of giant, towering women with faces that glowered, and once you had seen them, you looked more closely at Harriet herself: her light chatter seemed, then, less light. She was queer but she was serious. She shared her home on the Via Gregoriana with another sculptor, Emma Stebbins, a writer called Matilda Hays, whom everyone called Matthew, and the actress Charlotte Cushman, who recited Shakespeare at every opportunity, and who lounged on sofas even when everyone else was sitting up straight.

There was Mr Robert Browning, poet, and his wife, Elizabeth, better poet, who were permanently in Florence, but often in Rome; the husband a little dreary, you thought, and who once fell asleep while you were talking to him, but the wife positively other-worldly, an invalid and a genius who talked quite passionately about the power of spirit-rapping and the remarkable achievements of spiritual mediums.

And then there was the other person, the specific person. You met him on your first full day in Rome. It was Carnival time, and Mr Story had arranged a balcony for you overlooking the Corso, from where you could watch the procession of costumes and masks and dancing. You and the girls were dropping nosegays of camellias and confetti, little pea-sized balls of lime, onto the crowd below, and gentlemen in the procession were in turn tossing bouquets up to you, so that everything about you – hair, feet, skirts – was covered in petals. The scene below

23

was blurry with pink and red flowers, and Meta and Marianne were thrilled, reaching their hands out to clutch at what was thrown. You saw something fluttering through the air towards you, and reached out to catch it: a bunch of violets, and, attached to it by a fine string, a goldfinch. The little bird was struggling to free itself, its yellow wings quivering against your hands and wrists, its eyes bright and black. You snapped the tie off its leg and threw up your arms and watched as it darted away, above the rooftops of the Corso, until you could no longer see its red-masked face, its dark-and-gold-striped back. It was gone, and when you looked down, you saw directly beneath you a man standing still amongst the moving throng, staring up, and you said, 'Look, what a charming face!' and Mrs Story said, 'Oh, that's Charles Eliot Norton.'

'How shall I get to you?' he called.

2013

Rue d'Aboukir

'How was your journey?'

'Fine,' I say. 'Except, there was a sniffer.'

Max and I are in a taxi from the Gare du Nord to his apartment, and it is phenomenally awkward. We are sitting as far from each other as is possible in the back seat; I am clinging to the handle on the door, my legs crossed away from him. I stare out at the bistros that spill onto the street under red awnings, at tourists walking single file down narrow pavements, at mopeds weaving between the cars and the green crosses of pharmacies illuminating street corners.

By the end of our year together in Boston, Max and I were used to being almost constantly in each other's company, but here, in Paris, neither of us is able to think of a single thing to say. I consider making my declaration at once, just to fill the silence.

I realize that I have never actually been inside a place where Max lives: in Boston we always met in cafes, restaurants, never at our houses. He would collect me from my apartment sometimes, pulling up outside in his little grey car, but I never asked him in. He never even mentioned his place except to say, when asked, that it was in the Back Bay. Even the car, he insisted, was not his. Once I had said, sounding more accusatory than I intended, 'You have a nice car,' by which I meant, 'You have had a whole life before I met you and I don't know much about it. I do not know how you came to acquire this little grey car,' but he replied, quietly, 'It belongs to my brother.'

The idea of sharing a flat, a bathroom, of seeing the room where he sleeps, feels unprecedented and intimate. The knee-patting incident comes back to me, as does the excruciating embarrassment of my 'I've had feelings for you all year' email, and I become very aware of how I am sitting. I cross my legs even more tightly, and grip my knees. This whole visit seems, now that it is underway, wildly inappropriate.

Max's mind, it seems, has turned to the same thing. 'I've made up the bed for you,' he says. 'I'll take the couch.'

'No, no, really, it's fine,' I say. 'I can't kick you out of your own bed. I can sleep anywhere. I'm happy on the sofa.'

'Of course you're not going to sleep on the couch!' he says.

I wonder how long we can keep this up. We are sitting in traffic. It is beginning to get dark. The road ahead of us is glowing with red tail lights.

'I'll take the sofa,' I say.

The entrance to number 35, Rue d'Aboukir, is a small green door cut into an enormous green door. Max pushes it open and holds it while I step through into the stone hallway. The apartment is on the fourth floor, and

I climb the stairs, conscious that Max is close behind me, dragging my case up after him. As we near the top, my thighs start to burn. I'm embarrassed by my breathlessness; I try to suppress my panting. When we reach the fourth-floor landing and the narrow black door that leads to Max's apartment, we are both pink-faced and, while he fiddles with the keys, I go to the window, trying to collect myself. Below is a small courtyard, surrounded by shutters and boxes of geraniums, blots of red against the grey stone. I hear the click of the lock turning and Max says, 'Ah ha!' He opens the door and slides my luggage over the threshold.

Max's apartment is not, of course, really Max's. He is sub-renting it from someone he found online: a ballerina called Shu, who is touring with her company in South America. So, now, when I pad around the kitchen, looking at framed prints of inspirational quotes on the walls, and neatly stacked white crockery, it is not Max's private life I glimpse, but Shu's. On a shelf is a stack of notes from her boyfriend, mostly inconsequential – 'Love you Shu baby, have a good day!' – but archived nonetheless, under a seashell used as a paperweight. Magnets in the shape of ballet shoes hold up postcards on the fridge.

'The bedroom's through here,' Max says, lifting my case and disappearing with it through a doorway. I follow and watch as he sets it down beside the bed. Stacked against the wall are piles of books that I know are his and not Shu's because the collection comprises, almost entirely, books I love, and books I feel bad for not having read yet. Along the far wall there is an open clothes rail, from which Max's shirts hang in a row, and I have been so hyper-aware of Max for so long that I recognize each one and feel warm towards them, as though they are old friends. They are a line of past and future Maxes, waiting to come to life.

He moves back to the living room, and again I go after him, bringing my case with me. I put it next to the sofa. Max gets wine from the fridge. He points a remote at a speaker and music starts playing. He digs a corkscrew out of a drawer and begins to twist it into the cork.

I feel a sudden surge of glee to be there, with him, listening to music, about to drink wine.

'I'm so happy I came,' I say. 'I'm so happy to see you.'

There's a pause and then Max says, 'Me too,' without looking up from the wine bottle. It sounds so unconvincing and restrained that I blush and feel stupid, immature, too giddy. I retreat into the bathroom.

There is a rusting shower head poised over a tiny tub, and a sink squeezed in between the bath and the toilet. Max's shaving things are balanced next to the taps, and there are still little flecks of black stubble dotting the white enamel. The tap splutters when I turn it on, and the hairs swirl towards the plughole. There is no mirror above the sink into which I can glare and give myself a pep talk, so instead I scowl at the pattern of pale blue swirls on white tiles, and take several deep breaths, and rehearse for the hundredth time my declaration. *I can't be your friend any more.* I hear his footsteps in the other room, crossing the floor. *I have to fall out of love with you.* The clink of a glass being set down on the table top. More footsteps on the creaking boards. *And if I'm going to do that, I can't be your friend.*

When I come out, Max is standing at the window, looking down at the street. He is still, only moving to take occasional sips of wine, and I pause in the doorway to watch him. I have spent a lot of time, this past year, watching Max. One of our classmates at BU once confronted me about my feelings for him, and when I asked her how she knew, she said, 'Because you gaze at him, *longingly*, in class.' I was mortified. Now, while Max's back is turned, I indulge in a long gulp of a stare.

Thick black hair that flicks in several directions at once, with strands of light grey through it that remind me, whenever I notice, that I have no idea how old he is. The back of his neck, brown after a Massachusetts summer spent surfing, dips behind a checked blue collar. He is solid underneath his shirt, with wide swimmer's shoulders, and I have always loved the contrast between this, his breadth and bulk, and the way he inhabits space so gently. He is light-footed; his movements are small, apologetic; he is always careful about what he does with his hands, his feet, his eyes. He lifts his glass to his mouth and his sleeve falls back from his wrist, and I am just admiring the reassuring thickness of his forearm, the curve of muscle over bone, when he turns and sees me watching him.

He smiles. 'Maybe we should go out,' he says.

'We should,' I say. We must. I need to get out of this apartment, away from the music and the glass of wine meant for me that is sitting untouched on the table and the window that frames the man I love as though he were made just to stand in it. I need to leave because I have to make my declaration, and I am so breathlessly lustful in this moment that I can no longer remember the gist of it, let alone the words.

Outside, I remember that we are in Paris. Two hours on the train and just like that: a new country. It is so different from London, and yet, compared to America, so reassuringly European, that I am briefly disoriented as we walk down Rue d'Aboukir. The road is straight and quiet, punctuated with gaping doorways and occasional shopfronts. Right at the end, just before the street opens out onto the Place des Victoires, is a taxidermist's shop, the proprietor of which seems to specialize in creating chimera. The window presents a row of white mice with butterfly wings, a hawk with the head of an otter, a monkey with a bushy, white-tipped fox's tail. The face of a polar bear bursts through an arrangement of parrots. Further back in the display, a raven holds a key in its mouth.

After dinner, we walk through the gardens of the Palais Royal, past the Ritz (closed for renovations; a banner on the scaffolding reads, 'A Legend in Progress'), and then into the Tuileries, which are doused in orange light that rests on the edges of fallen leaves and rippled puddles. We make our way down walkways lined with foliage and suddenly, Max grabs my arm.

I jump. 'What is it?'

Max says nothing for a second, and then, 'I thought there was someone in the bushes.'

I peer into the empty flower bed beside the path. 'I don't think there is.'

But he doesn't let go of me. We carry on, arm in arm, and I am pathetically grateful for the gesture, knowing, as I do, that it is for my sake, that he knows how happy I feel walking like this, even when my shoulder begins to cramp because I am bending weirdly to fit under his arm.

We cross the river on the Pont des Arts, its walls bristling with locks attached by couples convinced, in a way I can't imagine, that their love is eternal enough to warrant commemoration on a French monument. At the end of the bridge, ridiculously, there is a newlywed couple doing a photoshoot. The bride is wearing an enormous white ball gown that draws in light from the streetlamps. The groom stands beside her, hand on her waist, and beams towards the crouching photographer. I start to laugh at the awkwardness of everything – of me, and Max, and this obnoxiously romantic city doing everything it can to highlight our inadequacies – but when I peer up at Max he looks stricken, the way he did that day in the parking lot in the rain, just before he got in the car. He is not laughing.

'I need to tell you something,' I say.

'OK,' says Max, and his face is stricken, stricken, stricken.

I take a breath. 'I . . .' *Do it. Say it.* 'I . . .' *No words.* So: 'I'm really happy to be here.'

'Yes,' he says, looking concerned still. 'Me too.'

The stricken face happens again and again. He makes it at the makeshift bar on the banks of the Seine where we stop for a drink. He makes it outside the Shakespeare and Company bookshop: it is late and the shop has closed, but there is enough light from the street to see the over-stacked shelves and the hand-painted sign: *Be not inhospitable to strangers lest they be angels in disguise.* When I turn to point this out to Max, there it is again: this expression of near-panic, his forehead creased, his lips unset, as though unsure what word to form. It happens on some stone steps near Saint-Germain-des-Prés, and again outside Notre-Dame, and again when we return to Rue d'Aboukir and pause for another look at the taxidermist's macabre display.

He knows, I think. *He knows about my declaration. Of course he does. He senses it is coming, and is conflicted: relieved that I am drawing a line under my infatuation, sad to lose a friend.*

Little green door inside the big green door. We climb the stairs and Max fumbles with the lock again and I brace myself for another round of squabbling about who takes the sofa, and when we get inside he makes his stricken face and says, 'I'm going to try something, OK?' and kisses me, and then we both take the bed.

2013

'I never get over to you': Unreachable Americas and the Idea of Home in the Letters and Fiction of Elizabeth Gaskell

'"Sometimes I dream I am in America, but it always looks like home, which I know it is not," Elizabeth Gaskell wrote to her American friend Charles Eliot Norton in 1860. To Edward Hale, another American acquaintance, she described America as "like the moon; I am sure it is somewhere, but quite untouchable in this mortal state." Gaskell's letters make repeated attempts to describe her relationship to America: a place she read about, whose citizens she knew as friends, but which she never visited herself. America emerges in these accounts as a distant, inconceivable place, whose existence is as undeniable as the moon's, but which is so far away as to exist, nonetheless, in the realm of the imaginary. "Sometimes I dream I go over to Boston," she wrote, again to Norton, in the year of her death, "but, I always pass into such a cold thick damp fog on leaving the river at Liverpool that I never get over to you." She draws a parallel between the imaginative and the physical journey: her inability to reach Boston in her dream is figured as an aborted sea voyage, a ship lost in fog.'

I have a distinct sense, as I speak, that I am losing the room. There is a muffled, restless noise coming from the group of people who are sitting around a horseshoe of desks, watching me. Legs are crossed and uncrossed, pens fiddled with, pages turned. There are a few paper plates of crisps being passed around, and whenever I pause, someone takes the opportunity to grab a handful.

I press on. 'Gaskell describes herself as "homesick" for America and the American spaces inhabited by her friends: "as if I had seen them once, and yearned to see them again." So, the question my research will ask is: What does it mean to be homesick for an imaginary place? Where does Gaskell locate herself, as an artist, if she insists on a homeland she never reached?'

Behind me on a screen is a PowerPoint slide depicting the original title page of a Gaskell novella called *The Moorland Cottage*: it includes an illustration of a group of people staring bleakly into a fireplace, as though expecting it to produce some sort of spectacle. Yesterday, when I put this presentation together, it all seemed quite moving: Gaskell's yearning for the New World, her inability to reach it even in her dreams, the sad story of *The Moorland Cottage* in which a troubled English boy sets sail to start a new life, to make a new home, in America, but instead drowns when his ship sinks near Wales. I thought that people would be instantly touched, as I am all the time, by the words and stories of Mrs Gaskell.

Instead, the faces looking back at me from the rest of

the room appear unmoved. They belong to the new cohort of doctoral students in the English department of King's College London. For the first year of our Ph.D. careers, we are required to attend a weekly meeting, termed, intimidatingly, the 'doctoral seminar', in which each student will present their proposed research project to the group.

So far in the seminar series we have seen presentations on:

— [Un]realism and [Hyper]realism in the Work of
  J. G. Ballard
— Katherine Mansfield, the Form of the Short Story
  and the Tyrannies of Female Fashion
— The Role of the Doorstep in the Fiction of Charles
  Dickens

My presentation is, at best, a guess: I have no clear idea what my thesis is going to be about. The proposal I wrote when I applied to King's focused vaguely on the idea of 'imaginary Americas' in the work of British writers who had never actually been to America. I was interested, I wrote, in the way these writers projected their desires and fears onto the blank canvas of the out-of-reach New World. After my year studying in Boston, the idea of longing for America seemed compelling. Writing about people writing about America would be an excuse to explore my own yearning for Max, and for the place in which I met and fell in love with him. I, too, pine for America.

Last week, however, I visited Max in Paris and before I could make my friendship-ending declaration to him, he made a different kind of declaration to me, which was, in summary: *I love you*. Since getting back to London I have been giddy and confused, replaying over and over the moment of discovery and its aftermath – the kiss, the bed, the *I love you*, the jubilantly sleepless nights and the following days we spent stumbling around the city clinging onto each other in a lustful mania – and now I am even less certain than I was before that my Ph.D. should be about yearning. Thirsting is not as interesting as it used to be. Longing is no longer relevant. I am in London and Max is in Paris and I have nothing left for which to yearn.

To complicate matters further, when I actually got around to putting together my presentation, I realized that the only example I knew of a British writer imagining America without going there is Mrs Gaskell, so it is Mrs Gaskell and only Mrs Gaskell that I discuss. Three minutes into my presentation, it is apparent to everyone here that a few letters, two novellas and some scattered references towards the end of a couple of novels is not enough material for a thesis.

After the presentation, the Q&A. I have been dreading it: my ignorance and guesswork could be so easily exposed. I don't, yet, know very much at all about unreachable Americas and the idea of home in the letters and fiction of Elizabeth Gaskell, and it would take only the very gentlest of questioning to make this apparent. That said, at the previous three seminars, the Q&A has rarely been focused enough to expose anyone or anything. Rather, it has been an excuse for other people to ask why the presenter has not considered the thing that they themselves have decided to research, which is obviously the most important angle to be taken on any writer, any subject, anything, always. Based on this evidence, I can anticipate interrogation along the following lines:

— From the lanky boy who reeks of cigarettes and writes on J. G. Ballard: Have you considered the role of un- and hyper-realism in Gaskell's portrayals of America?
— From the doorsteps-in-Dickens girl, who has a tattoo of Dickens' signature scrawled along the inside of her forearm: What role do you feel the notion of the liminal, the threshold, plays in Gaskell's writing? Could you see the form of the letter, which crosses between real and imaginary spaces, as a kind of doorstep? Did Elizabeth Gaskell ever write about doors?
— We may also cover, according to the various research projects represented in the room, Gaskell and *the tyrannies of female fashion*; Gaskell and *industrial coal mining*; Gaskell and *the narration of political divisions and civil unrest that might be seen to anticipate the Israel–Palestine conflict*. And so on.

The questions come, more or less ridiculous. My stock response each time is to write busily in my notebook and say, 'That's interesting. Yes, I'll look into that. Thank you.' None of them results in the anticipated humiliation, and it feels as though I am dodging knives thrown at my head, like some kind of academic ninja. I am even able to answer, moderately competently, a query about the reasons Gaskell never did go to America: she was married, she had four daughters and a frantically busy career. It seems, after all, I had nothing to fear. Perhaps I really do know what I am talking about.

Then, the professor, who has been tilting back in his chair silently until now, rocks forward and lands at the table with a thud. He is a specialist in nineteenth-century literature, and has written papers on Gaskell, and I am therefore hoping that he will look kindly on me. We are allies, united by mutual respect for our subject.

'I think, Nell, there may be a slight misreading underpinning your analysis,' he says.

He looks formidably serious, and I can feel blood rushing to my cheeks: a blush that proceeds to descend, like paint dripping, down my neck and under the collar of my shirt.

'Oh?' I say. I try my best to appear unruffled, composed. My pen is raised, ready to note something down as I offer my stock response.

'The quote you gave, in which Gaskell dreams of America and finds that it looks like *home*.'

'Yes?' I have the impression the professor is enjoying dragging this out.

'I think, if you look carefully, you'll realize that it does not in fact say "home" in that letter. It says "Rome". It says, "Sometimes I dream I am in America, but it always looks like *Rome*."'

I scribble in my notebook furiously. 'Oh, that's really interesting,' I say. 'Thank you. I'll look into that.'

1857

Goldfinch

It was as crowded on the balcony as it looked in the street below. There were so many of you squeezed in together, elbow to elbow, that when Mr Norton finally arrived, you all had to shuffle around awkwardly. You had watched him disappear beneath you, after Mrs Story had called down instructions for how to get up, and there had been a disconcertingly long wait for him to reappear. You had craned your neck over the iron railings to see whether he was stuck at the door, but had only managed to feel the rush of air as a bouquet flew past your face, and see the roofs of carriages strewn with flowers passing below. You sat back down and waited. Then you heard, behind you, the door click open and commotion as the crowded group reordered itself to accommodate another body.

You were shunted forwards until you were leaning right against the rail with Meta almost on your lap. Her hair brushed your face and you waved it away so that you could see, clearly, everything around you: the carnival, the street. You did not turn around. You felt suddenly self-conscious. Mr Norton must have heard you calling his face 'charming'. You thought people looked charming all the time, but you didn't usually proclaim it, loudly, from balconies. What was it about this person, this face, that had forced the words to erupt from you like that? You knew that later, soon even, you would find this funny, but for now you inwardly grimaced at yourself, your impulsiveness. You felt oddly aware of the back of your head, as though someone was staring at it.

'Ma, are you all right?' Marianne, the other side of Meta, was watching you.

You noticed that the carnival was beginning to die down. There was less to look at below.

Marianne, again: 'You've gone quiet, Ma.'

The crowd in the Corso was thinning. You wished for more noise. You heard, over the chatter of the other conversations around you on the balcony, Mrs Story saying, 'Oh, we all just adore her here,' and you wondered if she was talking to Mr Norton about you, and then frowned at your own presumption. 'She arrived only last night,' Mrs Story went on, and then you knew she really was talking about you.

'I am utterly devoted to *North and South*,' you heard a voice say in return: American, male, not belonging to any of the people you knew, and therefore belonging to Mr Norton.

You were never really shy, Mrs Gaskell, except for in this moment.

It was getting dark. Cool air was blowing into the city from the campagna, bringing with it smells of garlic and oil and wine from side-street kitchens, and Mr Story arranged for rugs to be brought up. You spread them over your knees, and Meta's and Marianne's, and gave both of your girls a squeeze. You wanted to show your daughters, and yourself, that you were happy to be there with them, that their company was the most important, that if you had nothing in the world but them, and Rome, and this little seat above the carnival, it would be more than enough. You were inexplicably unsettled, but you tried not to think too deeply, to acknowledge the feeling that bumped and knocked against your contentment: for all that you were lucky, for all that you already had, you still had this capacity to desire other things.

The flowers and confetti were gone, and there was a murmur from below, as children scurried around and candles were lit, and you picked up on a word repeated breathlessly on the street: *mocoletti*. You half-turned to ask Mr Story what it meant, but as you did so caught a glimpse of Mr Norton again, deep in conversation with Aubrey de Vere, a gloomy Irish poet who had tried, persistently, to convert you to Catholicism from the moment you arrived. You looked back at the street, and strained your ears to hear their conversation.

'My dear Mr de Vere,' said Mr Norton, 'I'm afraid I could not possibly bring myself to believe such a wholly nonsensical doctrine.'

As the night grew darker, more and more lights gathered below you: flickering wax tapers, thousands of them, and they began to move in a bright stream along the street. Each individual spark, when you focused on it, was tiny, but to look around you and take in the whole of it made you dizzy. Flame after flame joined the throng, and you opened your eyes wider and wider to see it, to fit it all in.

You remembered those evenings on the ship from Marseille, when the girls sang and you stared down into the phosphorescent water, and how you had felt the dinginess of Manchester life fall away from you like a discarded coat. How far away Manchester was now. But then, in thinking this, you thought of Manchester, and you felt a small knot of worry at the thought of life there going on as usual, of people reading your book and talking about you and saying goodness knows what behind your back.

You shook your head and returned to yourself. You felt the woollen weave of the rug on your knees, and the rub of your too-tight left shoe against your stockinged foot, the wind moving loose strands of your hair against your cheeks. You were there, on the balcony. You were hovering above a river of wavering, glinting *mocoletti*, and it was the loveliest thing you had ever seen, and to think about anything else was a waste. You wanted to fix it in your memory.

Without taking your eyes off the lights, you said to Meta, 'Isn't it just the loveliest thing?'

A second later you realized that Meta's chair was occupied by someone else, who turned to you with a bright smile and said, 'It truly is.'

You swallowed to hide your surprise, and then began to apologize. 'I thought you were my daughter. She was here just a moment ago.'

Mr Norton gestured to a group of figures who had

retreated from the cold evening air into the inner room. They were standing in a blaze of lamplight and amongst them you recognized Meta's hair and shoulders, the back of her head.

'Mrs Gaskell,' said Mr Norton, 'I have been trying all evening to reach you. So many of your friends have thrown themselves into my path, I thought I might never have the pleasure of introducing myself to one of my favourite writers.'

He told you his name, and you smiled, as though you hadn't known it all along. You never felt lost for words, and yet for a second, now, you truly were. Your heart was beating quickly, disturbed. All you could do was say it back to him. 'Mr Norton.'

'I don't mean to interrupt you,' he said. He looked sheepish, and half rose from his chair.

'No,' you said, 'no, you're not.'

You both looked down at the street, but the silence between you made you fidget, and after a few seconds, you said, 'Do you know, just before I saw you earlier, I caught a little goldfinch tied up with a bunch of flowers.'

'Did you really?'

'I did,' you said. 'I set him free, and he flew away over the roofs towards the Vatican.'

'Of course,' said Mr Norton. 'I expect he was late for Mass.'

2013

Q&A

'Can I ask you something?' I say.

Max is lying a little away from me in the bed, his back turned, and I reach out to run a finger down the lumps and grooves of his spine. He is drowsy, his shoulders swelling and sinking, but I am wide awake. It is early. The sun has found its way into Shu's bedroom and my mind is busy and ecstatic. This is my second visit to Paris, and even though two weeks have passed since that first extraordinary, never-expected turn of events in which Max and I became a couple, it still feels unreal. Shu's shuttered windows and the geraniums outside and the sheet that runs over Max's body and mine and the mattress between us: it all has an unreal quality, dreamlike, as though I haven't fully woken up yet.

'Sure,' says Max, turning over to look at me. The side of his face is creased from the pillow. His eyes are puffy. I am still not used to seeing him like this: guard down. 'Whatever you want.'

I have so many questions I'm not sure where to start. 'Something' is, in fact, 'many things', when it comes to what I do not yet know about Max.

'How old are you?'

He laughs. 'You don't know how old I am?'

'No! How would I?'

'I guess,' he says, 'that kind of thing normally just comes up.'

'Do you know how old I am?' I ask.

'You turn twenty-eight on December 22nd.'

'How—'

'You invited me to your twenty-seventh birthday party last year,' he says.

'You didn't come. And you didn't invite me to yours.'

'I'm thirty-five,' he says. 'I don't have birthday parties any more.'

Here is what I do know about Max: that he grew up in a suburb of Boston, in a big Irish Catholic family, and spent his summers at the beach on Cape Cod. His childhood was the solid, American kind that seems to me so exotic in films, the very vocabulary of which – Little League, Fourth of July, peanut butter and jelly – is foreign and exciting to my ear. Max always wanted to be a writer, but at some point during his late teenage years began to succumb to the gravitational pull of sensible choices: he decided to become a lawyer. It was a safe, practical option, and after a Master's degree in literature that he hoped would give him time to write, he went to law school, and from there to the litigation department of a large firm. He counted billable hours while sneaking sentences of the novels he hid in his desk, and, I gather, from a combination of hints and details that ring true in his short stories, growing increasingly miserable. And then, one day, he was done. He quit, went back to Boston, enrolled on the MFA. He was going to write full time. On campus, waiting for the first class to start, he sat on a bench overlooking the river and got out a book, which is when I first saw him, wearing a Red Sox baseball cap and reading Graham Greene's *The End of the Affair*.

A week earlier, in London, my friends come over and I take questions as though at a press conference. They have listened to tales of my lovesickness for the past year, have patiently analysed texts and emails from Max, and are full of generous excitement at recent developments, hungry for updates.

Louise is sitting on the floor; her husband, Frank, is behind her on the sofa. Her head tilts back into his lap, and he's playing with her hair. I remember seeing them do this before – how thoughtlessly they inhabit each other's space – and feeling incredulous that I could ever live that way, one half of a pair, and so casually, as though it were nothing extraordinary. But when I try to imagine it now, my head in Max's lap, his fingers in my hair, it seems suddenly easy.

'OK,' says Louise. 'Go. From the beginning.'

Holly is here, too, hugging her knees in an armchair. She has come straight from court, and her voice still has a hint of lawyerly cross-examination when she asks, 'So what did he say? Specifically. Did he just turn around and kiss you out of nowhere?'

'I mean, basically, yes.'

'And then he said he loved you.'

'Um, yes.'

'Just like that?'

'Just like that.'

She is about to continue her questioning when the bell rings and I get up to buzz in Izra, who is coming late from a parents' evening. She arrives with her arms full of marking and her eyes wide with a glazed, exhausted stare.

She sinks into a chair. 'What did I miss?'

'It's true love,' says Holly.

'Oh, is that all?'

Wine is poured; pizza is retrieved from the oven and divided up. I look around the room at my friends, women I have known since puberty. They are now, without exception, halves of couples, and our social circle has widened to include the men they have chosen to live with. Louise has Frank, Holly has Tom, Izra has Romaine; we have been a clique of seven for years. I have grown used to being the only single one, to entertaining them all with funny stories about bad dates and awkward one-night stands, like a foreign correspondent reporting from a far-off land they once visited but barely remember.

I have hoped that this would not always be the case, and expected pessimistically that it would be. The fact that I have found Max, that he is in love with me and says so all the time, makes me feel dizzy, jubilant, joyful, but also something quieter: I am relieved. I am not the solitary one any more.

'So when can we meet him?' asks Louise.

'Is he going to move to London?' asks Izra.

'Has he explained what made him change his mind about you?' asks Holly.

My Ph.D. supervisor is a woman called Joyce. She specializes in nineteenth-century American literature, and in particular, 'writing and friendship', which she talks about with a sort of brusque warmth. She has requested that I come and see her once every fortnight, so she can 'keep an eye on how things are going'.

'If you could send me your notes the day before each meeting, I can have a look and we can discuss them,' she said. I found this request comforting when she first made it, a reassurance that I would not be left to my own devices, to spiral out of control unsupervised. Now, at our third meeting, I find myself wishing that spiralling out of control unsupervised was, after all, an option.

We are sitting in her office on the seventh floor of the Virginia Woolf building at King's, and she is unimpressed. She shuffles printouts of my notes on the table between us, and flicks through the pages.

'There's not much here, Nell,' she says, 'for two weeks' work.'

'I've been reading,' I say, defensively. I look around the room, at the shelves stacked with books and with other students' finished theses: weighty tomes in blue binding with gold lettering down the spines.

'What have you been reading?'

What have I been reading? Text messages and emails from Max, mostly. 'Letters,' I say.

'I'd have liked to see more of a plan by this point in the term,' she says. 'I'd like to see a real sense of direction for your research.'

'I'm sorry. I've been . . . distracted, I guess,' I say.

She nods. 'What is it – a new boyfriend?' Her expression is both indulgent and disappointed as she folds her hands in her lap.

I want to cover my face. I'm blushing. In this room, in this building, I am supposed to be an intellectual, single -mindedly pursuing a deeper understanding of my subject. Instead, I am being outed as a light-weight: predictable, girlish, immature. 'Yes.'

'Right,' she says. 'The thing is, Nell, you won't get through this if you don't focus.'

'I know,' I say. 'I know.'

'A Ph.D. has to be an obsession. You have to have a monomania for it. Otherwise, it just won't happen. You won't get through three or four years of sitting by yourself in a library if it isn't absolutely the thing you want to be doing above all else. It has to be a labour of love.'

On my second visit to Paris, Max and I go to the Louvre, and despite everything, despite him, despite the art all around us and the city beyond, I am sulking. Joyce's warning has stayed with me, churning in the back of my mind: *a Ph.D. has to be a labour of love; otherwise, it just won't happen.* It has followed me all the way to St Pancras, onto the Eurostar, to Shu's apartment and, now, here, to the largest museum in the world.

'I don't know why I'm doing this Ph.D.,' I tell Max. 'Maybe it was a stupid idea.'

'What do you mean?'

'I'm not cut out to be an academic,' I say. 'I don't think I care enough about the sorts of things academics care about.' We are walking at speed through the high-ceilinged galleries, following signs, like everyone else, to the *Mona Lisa*. 'I like reading the writing of writers I love, and I like reading about writers I love. But I'm not sure I have anything additional to say about them. I think I'm more of an appreciative fan than a critic.'

'Then why do it?'

'I thought it would be good for my writing. And I thought it would help me get a job teaching at a university so I can write in the holidays and still get a mortgage. And I liked the idea of being an expert in something.'

'Those are all solid reasons.'

'But I'm over halfway through my first term,' I say, 'and I'm not even close to coming up with a subject, let alone being an expert.' The thought of spending the next three years in the library trying to make sense of scraps of writing by distant, long-dead people, trying to shape them into something coherent, is weighing heavily on me. 'I feel as though I know even less than when I started. I don't even know which country I'm writing about. Joyce says I need to have monomania for it, but I don't even feel like I have normal mania for it.'

Max stops in front of an Arcimboldo painting of a man's face assembled entirely from vegetables. 'Forget monomania,' he says. 'Just tell me what you like about it.

There must be something good about it – something that moves you.' Behind his head, the portrait's courgette nose protrudes.

I stop. I think. And then I tell Max about Mrs Gaskell.

When did I first start to love her? Was it when I was a teenager and read *Mary Barton* for the first time? Was it when, at the end of the novel, the characters leave Manchester, and cross the Atlantic to start a new life in a 'long low wooden house, with room enough and to spare', and the words washed around in my mind for weeks afterwards? It could have been then, or when I moved on to *North and South* or *Ruth* or *Cranford*, turning pages restlessly, wanting to get to the end without wanting them to be over.

Or was it when, as a Master's student, I found her books on the reading list for a module called, bleakly, 'Death in the Nineteenth Century'. I began an essay about her weird little novella, *Lois the Witch*, in which a young English girl travels to Salem, gets accused of witchcraft and is eventually hanged. The story of *Lois* seemed an odd choice of subject matter for an author I'd previously associated with domestic sagas and philanthropically motivated condition-of-England novels, but I loved it, and loved her for writing it.

As I worked on my essay, I wanted to get a sense of who Mrs Gaskell was, so I went to the Birkbeck Library in Russell Square, sat at a desk in front of the tall glass windows that overlooked the courtyard, and began reading her letters. And though I had seen the breadth of her imagination in her fiction, it was there, on the pages of her *Collected Correspondence*, that I really met Mrs Gaskell. *Do you know we are going to have a little kitten sent us from Paris, with long hair, and a very pretty face, and is called Cranford, can you guess why?* Every line of the letters fizzed with energy. Within a single paragraph, she covered what she planned to have for dinner and an international political incident, with some literary scandal thrown in for good measure. *I am afraid this letter is going to be what Dr Holland once called a letter of mine 'a heterogeneous mass of nonsense.' But that was before I wrote Mary B – he would not say so now.* Her slapdash punctuation and non-sequiturs and multiple exclamation marks belonged to a person too alive to be contained within the strictures of regular, nineteenth-century grammar. *Nature intended me for a gypsy-bachelor; that I am sure of. Not an old maid for they are particular & fidgety, and tidy, and punctual, – but a gypsy-bachelor.* It was probably then, I tell Max, that my love for her crystallized, became a fixture in my life.

I had never encountered a writer who could fill a page so entirely with herself, and haven't since. Mrs Gaskell is witty, and cutting, and sharp, and hilarious, and gossipy, and excitable, and dramatic, and above all, brimming with love for the people around her. *Do write us a long letter, we seem very far away from you; & I shan't begin to enjoy myself till I hear from you.* It oozes from those letters, that love; it reached me as soon as I began reading them, in the twenty-first century, in the Birkbeck College Library at Russell Square. I was caught up in her life almost instantly, in the hubbub of domesticity at her home on Plymouth Grove, in the ferocity with which she worked and fired off letters to her publisher and to other writers, and in the way she never seemed quite content with any of it: she played the role of wife and mother so very well, and so lovingly, but she was a 'gypsy bachelor' nonetheless.

She was always demanding long letters from her loved ones, and complaining if the replies she received were too short. I felt – still feel – a pang, something like lovesickness, when I think that Mrs Gaskell and I can't write to each other. We would write such good letters, I think. We would have so much to say.

When I imagine my ideal Ph.D. – the one that could actually be a labour of love, a monomania, a joy to write – it is one long letter to Mrs Gaskell.

By the time I finish explaining all of this to Max, we have reached the *Mona Lisa*. There is a crowd of tourists around the painting and we can't get close. I stand on tiptoes, trying to get a look, but all I see is the pale circle of a face repeated over and over on the screens of raised phones, taking pictures.

'Mrs Gaskell went to Rome,' I tell Max, as we wait to get to the front of the crowd. 'She met an American there, a man called Charles Eliot Norton, and he changed her life. They understood each other. They had this incredible connection. I think she felt free, liberated, with him and all these artists: British and American painters, and sculptors, and writers. I think she finally felt that she was among her people. It was transformative for her, to meet Norton, to be in Rome, to be treated as an equal by other artists.'

'And that interests you,' says Max. 'That moves you.'

'Yes.'

'So then write about it,' he says. 'Just write.'

When we finally get close to the painting, I look up into the face of the *Mona Lisa*. She meets my gaze and smiles, as though she has known the answer to my Ph.D. woes all along, and has been waiting for me to get there by myself.

Back in London after that second trip to Paris, I call Max on Skype. I am sitting on the floor of my room in Haggerston, computer on the bed. Max is at the table in Shu's apartment, with laundry drying behind him: the sheets that I was sleeping on only a night ago.

We are beginning to fall into a rhythm. There are the intense days when we are in the same city, when our bodies ache from too much sex and not enough sleep, and my mind fizzes over with things I want to say to him and things he has said to me. These are followed by the eerie quietness of separation: of being apart, sleeping alone, and nightly Skype calls. I am adjusting to this alternative, two-dimensional version of Max, his head contained neatly in a box on the screen, occasionally pixelated or out of sync with the sound.

When we are tired, and it is late, we don't speak, but

type to each other instead. I don't know why it is easier to type than to speak out loud, but it is, and I am bolder in writing than I am in speech. And so, after some back and forth about our days – my journey back to London, his work on a new story – I ask him something I haven't dared mention before.

Nell: I have another question for you.

Max (expression momentarily concerned, and then adjusted back to a smile): OK.

Nell: Do you remember that time in Boston, when I told you that I liked you? You said you weren't looking for a relationship. Why?

Max: I'm sorry I said that.

Nell: But why did you?

Max: Because . . . I was an idiot.

Nell: No but why?

[Pause. He begins to type – three rippling dots on the screen – then stops, then starts again.]

Max: I had just left this life where I was always working, doing work I hated, and I was truly, seriously miserable. And I did this crazy thing of giving it up to become a writer, and moved back to Boston, and I went back to school . . . When I started at BU it seemed I had bought myself all this

time – I felt as though I had ages to figure
out what my next move was. But then all
of a sudden it was summer and I had to
confront the future all over again. People
kept asking me: what next? And I didn't
know. I don't know. I'm writing, but I can't
know what will come of it. It just didn't
seem like the time to commit to something –
to someone. I knew I was coming to Paris,
but this isn't forever, and in a few months
I'll have to go back home and start earning
some money, you know?

> *Nell: OK.*

Max: OK?

> *Nell: But then, what has changed now?*
> *Doesn't all that still apply?*

Max: No. I realized it doesn't matter.
I want to be with you, and that's more
important than all those other things.
[Pause] Is that OK? Are you OK?

I don't type back. I feel suddenly panic-stricken. Since
Max first kissed me, I have been remarkably sanguine
about our relationship, have come to accept it as a thing
that is rightfully mine, and that cannot be taken away. I
scan back over our conversation; it is littered with question marks, and they make me feel sick. I catch sight of
my face in the little box on the top right of the screen:
pale and frowning.

'Hey,' Max says, switching to speaking. 'I bought you something today.'

I type, 'You did?' and then feel stupid and repeat it out loud. 'You did?'

He leans out of shot for a moment, then returns, holding up a little red book. It is old, the fabric of the cover fraying in one corner, revealing the brown board beneath.

'Hold it still,' I say. 'I can't read the title.'

When the gold lettering comes into focus, I read: '*Anglistica & Americana*. What is that?'

He opens to the title page: *Letters of Mrs Gaskell and Charles Eliot Norton, 1855–1865.*

'I was just browsing in a market stall earlier, and there it was,' he says, 'just waiting for me to find it. Have you read them before, the letters?'

'I've read some of hers to him,' I say, 'but not his to her.'

Max puts the book down out of sight, and smiles. 'You'll like them. I read them this afternoon,' he says, and then, still smiling, but more quietly, 'I didn't realize they would be love letters. You didn't tell me they were in love.'

2013

Basic Accounting for Ph.D. Students

How to explain desire? In particular, how to explain desire in Mrs Gaskell, a person I have always imagined, unquestioningly, as somehow asexual? She seems, in my vision of her, mumsy, reassuring. After discovering her in her letters, I returned to the novels with new devotion: I have spent rainy days in cafes reading *Cranford*, nights curled up at home with the BBC adaptation of *North and South* playing on my laptop. She is cosy and comforting. And yet, as I read her letters, it is becoming increasingly apparent to me that she did desire things, people. She desired Charles Eliot Norton.

Mrs Gaskell. There is something determinedly unsexy about that 'Mrs': proper, old-fashioned. I have always hated it on principle. We don't insist on Mr Dickens, Mr Thackeray, Mr Trollope. And yet I can't help but use it, when I talk about her. When I consider her as an author, only, rather than a person, she is simply 'Gaskell'; in my academic writing she sometimes becomes 'Elizabeth Gaskell', if I need to distinguish her from other Gaskells in the same paragraph: William, Meta, Marianne. And to those other Gaskells, I learn from reading more of her correspondence, she was not in fact 'Elizabeth', but 'Lily'.

Still, it is 'Mrs Gaskell' I come back to, in general usage; out of habit, I suppose, and fondness: a desire to keep her soothing presence close.

It seems sacrilegious, at very least disrespectful, to imagine her as she must have been: a sexual being, desirous as we all are of other people, of other people's bodies.

The Rare Books and Music Reading Room at the British Library is an L-shaped space, with the exit at one end and the Issue and Returns desk around the corner. The floor is taken up with blocks of desks, each with its own lamp and place mat that details the rules: no food, no water, no pens, no coats, no Post-it notes. At the very top of the high ceiling there are windows that let in the slightest suggestion of natural light. It is a place of very few distractions; it would take severe effort just to tell if the weather outside had changed.

I am sitting at the back, where I sit almost every day, holding a copy of a Mrs Gaskell book called *A Dark Night's Work*. In it, a young woman, after becoming entangled in a somewhat melodramatic murder plot in England, goes on holiday to Rome. There, from a balcony overlooking the Corso during the carnival, she sees the young man who will go on to become her husband. The book is so old that the glue on its spine disintegrates into dust when I turn the pages. But I am not really turning the pages. In this hushed, well-lit space of contemplation, absent of external distractions, I find myself constantly distracted. For every ten minutes I spend reading and re-reading the balcony scene in *A Dark Night's Work*, or researching the role of Rome as a triangulating point of encounter in transatlantic literary dialogues, I spend twenty thinking about Max. I am doing better with work after our conversation in the Louvre, but still, if I have a monomania, as Joyce described, it is clear that it is not about my research.

The Max obsession is nothing new, of course, but its focus has changed. Whereas once my thoughts rotated around an axis of self-pity and wounded ego, they are now sexual, and, frustratingly, logistical. Even thinking about his name makes my stomach squirm and my mind turn at once to the apartment on the Rue d'Aboukir, to the low bed in the room that looks over the courtyard, to Max's hands and mouth and body. Then I begin, frantically, to plan how to get back to Paris. And then I return, over and over, to the same theme: seeing Max costs money, and it costs time. The train is expensive. Term has not yet ended, and I should be glued to my seat in the reading room. Paris is supposed to be a luxury, a holiday, and whereas once a trip would be planned for months and anticipated and researched, now my instinct is to dash to St Pancras at a moment's notice. It is only nine minutes' walk from where I sit in Rare Books to the Eurostar ticket office – a fact I think about approximately three times an hour.

Since my first visit, I have been back twice. Max has come to London, too, and met Holly and Izra and Louise, but the room I am renting in Haggerston is barely big enough to contain a full-size bed, let alone two adults and their belongings, and I'm aware that Max is older than me, and a little past the house-sharing, laundry-everywhere, washing-up-left-in-the-sink phase of life. My housemates are too present and too observant for it not to be embarrassing when Max and I emerge from my room in the middle of the afternoon, hair awry, faces red, both a little sweaty.

And besides, Haggerston is fine, but it's not Paris. It's not the second *arrondissement*, where we drink espressos in the morning at a cafe called Père et Fils, and from where we walk to the Seine every night to watch the lights of the bridges drop into the water. London feels quotidian and dull. The drizzly, crowded, subdued texture of it, which I missed so much when I was living in Boston, is suddenly drab.

I am reading about Rome – *I dream I am in America, but it always looks like* Rome – and in between fantasies of Max, and financial calculations, I am getting to know the members of the group of British and American artists who lived there in the middle of the nineteenth century, the ones Mrs Gaskell met and loved. They worked together, side by side: American sculptor Harriet Hosmer next door to British sculptor John Gibson; British poet Robert Browning learning to model clay in the studio of American William Wetmore Story; Emelyn Story at a dinner party telling ghost stories Mrs Gaskell had originally written to her, and which then found their way into Nathaniel Hawthorne's novels. Every Friday night, Story held an open house where the expatriate artists and writers gathered to talk and eat and collaborate. Their buzzing conversation, Henry James wrote, filled the rooms with a golden glow like electric light. They had ideas. They discussed them. They made art. They wrote. Harriet Hosmer once invited the Brownings to her studio to take a cast of their hands, clasped together, and it gives me a sense of panicked yearning to imagine it: how wonderful it must have been to be surrounded by like-minded friends, and somehow also to be so productive.

After my meltdown about my Ph.D., Max and I instigated formal writing hours while we were together, during which we would work, he on his fiction and I my thesis, and we would not touch each other at all, not even a little bit. We spent a tense afternoon at the table in Shu's apartment. I made half-hearted notes on an article about Mazzini and the unification of Italy while Max frowned at his laptop and occasionally tapped the keys. And then I crossed my legs, and as I did so my foot just happened to brush against his knee, and without looking up he sank a little lower in his chair so that my calf slid along his thigh, and then it was all over and we left the table, pulling clumsily at each other's clothes and panting, as though we hadn't been together in weeks.

The next day we filled out applications to use the library at the Institut de France: fiercely formal, all dark wood and golden chandeliers. But there we were assigned desks next to each other and it took only an hour or so before our knees were touching as we wrote, and though I kept typing, I was so aroused and distracted by the closeness of Max, by the very idea of him, that the next time I opened my laptop I realized the page I'd been working on was a mess of half-thought-through observations on American interpretations of Risorgimento politics in art, and increasingly desperate notes to Max: *Expatriate view of Italian politics . . . a polite distance and/or through an artistic lens . . . Shall we go soon? . . . the idea of Rome, both ancient and modern – a stimulus for questions re. collaboration/independence . . . autonomy? . . . Let's go! I can't concentrate! . . . nineteenth-century debate re. national identity in Italy and US relates to expatriate identity . . . the metaphor of the city state . . . I want you . . . Let's just give up and go home . . . etc.*

Now, in my notebook, interspersed between notes on my reading, I am jotting down numbers, and lists of pros and cons: the amount I am paid, monthly, in a stipend from King's versus the cost of train tickets to Paris; the value of staying in London and getting on with my research versus the hedonistic glee of seeing Max again. Sometimes the conclusion seems clear: I should travel less, spend less, see Max less, work more. But on other days I am awash with desire and then, somehow, nothing adds up after all.

I attend a lecture on Victorian attitudes to marriage. It takes place in a cramped, book-lined room at Birkbeck College, where the audience is arranged in rows of folding chairs that creak at the slightest fidget, and the speaker is leaning on a lectern that tilts to the left. His papers keep sliding off and he catches them each time, then delivers the rest of the lecture with one hand firmly pinning them down.

He covers religion, child-rearing, private and public spheres and the notion of the perfect wife. And then, in passing, he says, 'The Victorians, generally speaking, had less sex than people in the eighteenth, and in the twentieth and twenty-first centuries.' I had been listening only partially until that moment – my mind drifting, persistently and repeatedly, to the Rue d'Aboukir where Max would be, at that moment, hard at work on his writing – but this suggestion cuts through my fantasies.

I am intrigued and oddly upset by the idea, and when the time comes to ask questions, I raise my hand.

'I'm interested in your assertion that the Victorians had less sex,' I say, and there are a few uneasy titters from some undergraduates behind me. 'How do you know that? How can we tell that?'

The speaker is patient, and a little amused, and gives a long, unsatisfactory answer. I listen and nod and know it would be thoroughly awkward to press the point any further, but can't help but feel . . . what? Unconvinced? Disappointed?

Why do I care, I wonder, as I stomp the now-familiar path between Russell Square and the British Library. It's a weird thing to care about. For all that the lecturer said about birth rates and prostitution and sexually transmitted diseases, it seems so much more likely, doesn't it, that we simply struggle to imagine these people, whose novels tended to avoid discussing sex directly, and whose names we have known since we were children, getting naked together and doing we-all-know-what just as exuberantly and filthily and weirdly as every other generation?

Here is how I am attempting to balance my life. I dissect Max's body, and for its sake, I set myself tasks, as though it could be as simple, as neat, as a transaction. Perhaps I won't feel so uneasy, so greedy and distracted, if I can use my desire to exercise some self-control in other areas of my life.

For Max's tousled black hair, I will write five hundred words on the costs of living for expatriate artists in Rome. For the crease in his upper lip, I'll send an update on my progress to Joyce. For his shoulders, I'll read an exceedingly dry article on subjectivity, biography and the portrayal of William Wetmore Story and his friends in Henry James' *William Wetmore Story and His Friends*. For his back, I'll walk home through driving rain, rather than replace the umbrella I left beside my table in the graduate student lounge, and which was gone by the time I went back for it.

This is all well and romantic and good until the crushing boredom of reading yet another argument about the influence of Robert Browning's dramatic monologues on William Wetmore Story's statues makes me truly question the value of, say, Max's chin, or his waist, or his knees.

———

Because Mrs Gaskell never wrote about her desire directly, I have to search for it in places it might not be. I read between the lines, and when I see nothing there, I crowbar them further apart and look again.

Take this, for example, which she wrote to Norton in 1861, four years after they both left Italy, four years before she died:

> Oh! Don't you long to go back to Rome. Meta and I were so talking about you, and Rome and America yesterday, the Pamphile Doria gardens especially and about your face as we first saw it, – and this morning comes your letter.

I can read these sentences and write, *the swirling syntax here indicates a geography of memory that circles around Norton: contained in the intimacy of the initial 'you' is the global sweep of 'Rome and America', the relative specificity of the gardens, and in sharper focus still, the body of Norton – 'your face as we first saw it'. Finally, the attention turns to the immediate physical object of the letter: a tangible connection between Norton's body and Gaskell's own, and which thus itself becomes a fetishized object of desire.*

I cannot say: [Mrs] [Elizabeth / Lily?] Gaskell's reaction to Charles Eliot Norton's physicality was likewise physical. She was attracted to him. His face 'as she first saw it' was an object of desire that made her cry out in the street, and the memory of which, years later, made her heart thud and her cheeks flush. She wanted to touch him. She ached for him, the way I ache for Max when I am away from him in London, when I am hurtling towards him on the expensive train, when I am sitting beside him, knee against his, in the library of the Institut de France.

Other people's desires, I suppose, are always hard to comprehend. I have watched friends in the past fall in love and lust with people who seemed formidably undesirable. Former passions of my own – for men and women who once struck me as sexually irresistible – seem overblown and embarrassing with hindsight. Desire is private and incomprehensible, confined to specific bodies in specific times. Across centuries and filtered through letters and novels, it is immaterial and ahistorical, suggested, only hinted at. And yet, as I read and re-read Mrs Gaskell's writing to and about Norton, I can't help thinking it is palpable for all that.

In the Rare Books Reading Room, I am listlessly going over my writing from the day before when an email arrives in my university inbox. 'The Institute of Psychiatry would like to invite eligible students to take part in a study we are conducting for the purpose of a Ph.D. project, which looks at the effects of temporarily decreasing your brain's dopamine activity on your body image, eating, and exercise behaviours. We are seeking female participants between the ages of 25 and 35. Participants will be compensated with £150 upon completion of the study.' It seems, in that moment, like a gift: instead of sitting there in that lifeless, airless room, I could do this other thing, which while not helping my Ph.D., would at least help somebody's, and for my trouble I'd be paid enough to buy a train ticket to Paris. For the first time in weeks, it seems as though something adds up.

1853

The Casting of *The Clasped Hands of Robert and Elizabeth Barrett Browning* by Harriet Hosmer

'Will you let me take a cast of your hands?'

Harriet Hosmer was sitting with Mr and Mrs Browning in one of the dining rooms at the Hôtel d'Angleterre, where a fire was lit and a young Italian man was waiting by the door, refreshing their coffee cups after each sip they took. She had been quiet for a while, listening to Elizabeth and Robert talk, watching the way they moved when they spoke.

'A cast?' said Elizabeth. She put down her cup and glanced at her fingers, splaying them out in front of her as though trying to judge whether or not she thought them worth preserving. From across the table, Harriet studied them too.

'It wouldn't take long,' Harriet said. 'The *formatore* will set the plaster, and I can sit with you while it dries. If we set ourselves up by the fire, just as we are now, it would be done in no time – a morning, maybe less. And I can see how it will be – quite lovely, the two hands clasped together just so.' She entwined her own hands in front of her face, as though greeting herself.

Robert, Elizabeth could see, was self-conscious. He had made fists, and half withdrawn them under his sleeves. But she knew that he liked the idea, despite himself. He liked anything that consolidated his view of himself as not just a poet but an artist. And he liked Hattie, too, with her soft, constant babble of ideas and stories. She was almost young enough, at twenty-three, to be his daughter, and he indulged and coddled her as though she was.

'Robert always longed to be a sculptor,' Elizabeth said.

Harriet brushed this off, as though it was obvious, and to Harriet, it probably was.

'It will represent,' said Harriet, loftily, 'the meeting of two great minds in marriage, and in their work. It will show what it is to be poets in love with one another and with Italy and with words.'

Robert snorted. 'You think people will take all that from a cast of my ugly paw?' He was trying to suppress a smile.

'Will you let me make the cast?' Harriet said, again.

'We will,' Elizabeth said, 'provided you will cast them. I will not sit for the *formatore*.'

If a person was going to touch her, and touch Robert, and most intimate of all, touch them both while they were touching each other, it could not be a stranger. There was something that made Elizabeth's skin crawl in the thought of the wet plaster being administered by a rough-fingered man; it would have to be Harriet herself, with her neat, quick hands.

'All right,' said Harriet. 'I'll do it.'

71

It was agreed. Elizabeth and Robert would go to Harriet's studio the next day.

When Robert and Elizabeth arrived at the address on the Via della Fontanella that Harriet had given them, nobody was there. Robert knocked, and when there was no reply, he pushed the door.

Inside the studio, they wandered between works in progress and finished pieces: a naked youth, all muscle and sinew, bending to hold back a dog; another, thrusting his groin forward as two enormous, topless nymphs slid robes off his shoulders. There was a model, still in the clay, of a young girl kissing a cherub. Her breasts were exposed and the crease between her thighs sharply cut. Elizabeth, embarrassed, turned to the canvases and books of loose papers that were stacked against the walls, and began to leaf through. In some there were sketches of places around the city that were instantly familiar – the ruins of the forum, Trajan's column – but mostly she found pictures of statues and models for statues, a catalogue of arms and thighs and necks and nipples and unabashed, flaccid penises. She slid the pages back between the cardboard covers.

They were in a cathedral of nudity, of bulging stone bodies, and when they came across a Venus, breasts displayed above a useless cloth that was draped over her arm and hid nothing at all, there was an awkwardness between them. The statue was dyed somehow, tinted in pink, fleshy hues that made the figure seem ready to blink, to pick up her robe and rearrange it over her shoulders to cover herself, and close her red lips around the apple she held in her left hand. The other statues, in their bare whiteness, seemed inert by comparison.

'I don't know where to look,' Elizabeth said, and Robert, who seemed relieved that the silence was broken, said, 'I would focus on the face, but even that seems a little indecent.' Elizabeth stared at the statue's expression: defiantly blank, a little bored.

'I wouldn't have imagined this from Harriet,' Elizabeth said, and at that moment Harriet herself put her head around a door at the back of the room.

'Oh, there you are.'

'Is this not where we are supposed to be?' asked Elizabeth, turning her attention at once to a bust of Helen of Troy, portraying only an elegant head and long neck, cut off neatly above the breasts.

'I'm through here,' said Harriet. 'This isn't my studio. It's Mr Gibson's.'

Harriet's room, at the back of Mr Gibson's studio, was a dusty, high-ceilinged cave. Marble chips crunched underfoot as they crossed the floor, in between Harriet's efforts at busts. The table tops, the clay models, everything was coated in a thick white powder. Robert ran his finger along a surface, and ground the dust between his fingers.

'Yes, sorry,' said Harriet. 'It's grimy in here. I've been experimenting with a new technique for polishing marble, but so far have only succeeded in making a tremendous mess.'

'It's a lovely room, Hattie,' said Elizabeth, turning to look at two female heads in marble: a serpent-haired Medusa and a modest, retiring Daphne.

'I'm no Mr Gibson, I know,' she said, patting the busts casually, as though they were dogs. 'This is just the beginning,' she said. 'I was very fond of my Medusa, until Mr Story came by and told me my snakes look like eels.'

'They don't look like eels,' said Elizabeth at once, but Harriet laughed.

'One day I'll make great women with real power. They will make you tremble just to look at them. But while I'm still learning I must satisfy myself with disembodiment. I am hard at work putting together the pieces of the human body, bit by bit. Head, neck, shoulders. Look here, this is a cast of my own foot, crooked toes and all. It's like a surgeon's theatre in here, these days. But soon I'll make a full woman and everybody will be embarrassed by her, as they are by Mr Gibson's.'

'Mr Gibson's statues are . . .' Robert paused, 'very detailed.'

'So will mine be,' said Harriet, sitting down heavily on a stool, 'so let's begin.' On the worktop in front of her, she had already mixed the wet plaster, and laid out the bandages.

First was the grease, lewd and frictionless, which Harriet slathered on Elizabeth's right hand. Elizabeth flinched.

It was cold in the studio, and the wet fat was a shock to her skin. Then, as Harriet glided her fingers across Elizabeth's palm, knuckles and joints, muttering, crossly, 'Don't be so tense,' she relaxed and gave up her hand to Hattie's rubbing.

'Now hold it up,' said Harriet. 'Keep it away from your clothes.'

Elizabeth sat awkwardly, arm aloft, as Harriet took Robert's hand and began the process again, scooping grease out of the tin and smearing it over the broad, bony back of his hand. She rubbed it all over his skin and wrist, and it was mesmerizing to watch, how quickly she worked, how easily her fingers moved over the shapes of Robert's body.

When the time came to take Robert's hand in hers, Elizabeth blushed. Her hand, coated in fat, felt rubbery and odd. When Robert's touched her, their palms slid against each other, their fingers interlaced and then slithered out of the grip. Harriet laughed and took hold of their wrists and arranged them as she wanted: Robert's large hand supporting Elizabeth's, which was bent just enough to expose bones and veins running along the back. Robert caught Elizabeth's eye, and she swallowed.

'There,' said Hattie, then, to Robert, 'but hold her harder. Hold her as though she were slipping away.' She began to apply the plaster in cold, wet strips, working over and around their grip, so gently and tenderly it seemed to Elizabeth that she was being swaddled.

Afterwards they sat in a strange silence, waiting for the cast to harden, Robert and Elizabeth stuck together, hand in hand, and Harriet beside them, reaching out occasionally to tap the plaster.

Harriet looked towards the empty fireplace and sighed. 'I'm sorry. I promised a fire but the girl didn't light it. I don't know why.'

Elizabeth shook her head, and even this movement made her aware of the solidifying grip of the cast on her hand. 'I'm not cold.'

'It will take longer to set,' said Harriet.

Inside the cast, Robert's hand twitched against Elizabeth's.

'We don't mind,' Elizabeth said, and when the time came for Hattie to get the knife and cautiously, gingerly, cut through the plaster right up to the surface of the skin, it felt too soon, as though she was sawing through something still underway, as though their hand-holding had only just begun.

2013

Body Study

Here's how it goes: the day before the study, I eat a pre-scribed diet that contains no protein, a lot of vegetables, and, oddly, a two-finger Kit-Kat; dinner is half a cucumber and a head of lettuce. The next morning, I present myself to a research lab adjoining King's College Hospital in Denmark Hill. On the walk from the bus stop, I pass two cafes, where people in the windows are nursing mugs and looking satisfied.

The lab itself, when I reach it, smells disconcertingly of coffee. While I wait to be seen, I distract myself from caffeine cravings by reading the posters on the waiting-room walls: 'Are you a twin or do you know a twin? Join 13,000 other identical and non-identical twins aged 16 and above already registered with TwinsUK'; 'Are you a WORRIER? We are looking for people aged 18–65 who tend to worry a lot about different topics, have normal or corrected-to-normal vision or hearing and are fluent in English'.

We would like to invite you to take part in a research study with human subjects. This study is being conducted for a Ph.D. in Psychology degree. You should only participate if you want to.

Please take time to read the following information carefully. Talk to others about the study if you wish.

This study is investigating the effects of temporarily decreasing your brain's dopamine activity on the way you feel about your body. The research involves reducing the availability of certain amino acids for entry into your brain. On the day of the study, you will ingest an amino acid drink that is selectively lacking in dopamine's precursors, which will cause a short-term reduction in your brain's dopamine activity.

Danielle, the Ph.D. student whose study this is, introduces herself in a soothing voice, as though she's worried I might have second thoughts and make a run for it. She escorts me into the main hospital building to have a blood sample taken, past patients being wheeled along on trolleys or in chairs, and an elderly man who stands motionless, looking blankly at a wall. She touches me on the arm occasionally to check I'm all right, and though I am perfectly well, in the echoey, sanitized hospital, I start to feel a bit pathetic, as though I really am ill.

As the technician sticks a needle in my arm and the syringe turns dark red, I remind myself why I am here, why I am doing this. With my free arm, I get out my phone and text Max, 'I am literally bleeding for you,' to which he responds, at once, 'You are a hero of our time,' and then, moments later, 'Take care. Love you. Don't do anything you don't want to.' It feels more awkward than I thought it would, being a test subject, giving up blood and data in exchange for money.

'What do you do?' Danielle asks, as we walk back towards the lab.

'I'm doing my Ph.D.,' I say.

'What in?'

'English Literature.'

'What's it about?'

I am feeling a bit woozy after the blood being taken, and without coffee. The words that come out of my mouth are, 'Dead people.'

Danielle smiles politely.

'I mean,' I say, 'Victorians. British and American writers and artists who lived in Rome in the middle of the nineteenth century. I just meant, they are dead, they aren't around to give blood and tell me what they're feeling.'

Danielle nods, but she is flipping through the papers in her folder as we walk and making little notes in biro. 'That's tough,' she says.

I've read through the study information, but I don't yet have a clear idea of how I'll be spending my day. The only thing I know is that there will be a phase, early on, called, ominously, 'drink ingestion'.

'Some people find the amino acid a bit tricky to get down,' Danielle says, filling a large plastic cup with water from the cooler. 'And some people can't keep it down. The best way to do it, I've found, is very slowly, through a straw. I'll leave you to it. Most people manage to get through the whole thing in about an hour.'

She sets the cup down on the table in front of me. Over it, she opens and empties large capsules, as though she is cracking eggs into cake mix. The powder from the pills doesn't dissolve in the water, but instead froths up and gives off a plastic-y, chemical smell. It looks like the foam left on tidelines of polluted beaches. She gets a straw and dunks it into the mixture, but it floats up to the top with the foam, and lies at an awkward angle across the top.

'Fill out the questionnaire,' Danielle says, patting a clipboard, 'and then do the drink, and I'll be back in an hour.'

In this booklet you will find statements people might use to describe their attitudes, opinions, interests, and other personal feelings. For each of the following questions, circle the number that best describes the way you usually or generally act or feel.

> 1 = Definitely false, 3 = Neither true nor false, or equally true or false, 5 = Definitely true.

I feel so connected to nature, everything is part of one living process.   1 2 3 4 5

When I meet a group of strangers, I am more shy than others.   1 2 3 4 5

I am more sentimental than most people.   1 2 3 4 5

I think that most things that are called miracles are just chance.   1 2 3 4 5

When someone hurts me in any way,
I try to get even.   1 2 3 4 5

My actions are determined largely by
influences outside my control.   1 2 3 4 5

I think I am a special person with a
special purpose.   1 2 3 4 5

Each day I take another step toward
my goals.   1 2 3 4 5

Please circle the number four, this is a
validity item.   1 2 3 4 5

I am a very ambitious person.   1 2 3 4 5

The next page is full of silhouettes of women in rows of ten. They begin narrow on the left-hand side and get gradually wider towards the right, like a 'march of progress' illustration charting weight gain instead of evolution. 'Please mark the silhouette that best represents your body shape,' the first line says, and I draw a cross under woman number five. Line two: 'Please mark how you wish to look'; I dither and then choose one slightly to the left of my first pick. Line three: 'Which is the most attractive silhouette?' I pick the same one as on the line above. Then, on the last line: 'Which is the most attractive silhouette to the opposite sex?' I think about Max, and riding a wave of smugness, revert to silhouette number five. Then, in a rush and before I can overthink it, I pick up the plastic cup of chemical froth, and down it.

I am suppressing the urge to vomit by gritting my teeth and clenching my throat, and Danielle is affixing sensors to my face. She sticks one just below my left eye, and another just above it, and a third on my neck. If I move too much, the wires tug on my skin, so I am sitting as still as I can. With a flourish, as though she is adding the finishing touches to some kind of art installation, she tucks headphones into my ears.

'I'm going to show you a series of images, and I want you to note down how interested you feel in them, OK?'

'Interested?' I ask.

'Yes,' she says, and doesn't offer further explanation. 'The sensors on your face are measuring your blinking, which is a startle response. Periodically throughout the next thirty minutes, you will be startled with a tone.'

I'm about to ask what she means by 'startled with a tone' when a shrill beep sounds in my ears, and I jump so hard the sensor wires pull taut.

'Like that,' Danielle says. 'It's a control measure.'

The images flashing up on the screen belong to four different categories: fat people, thin people, exercise equipment, and furniture. An obese man struggling to climb some stairs is followed by a rocking chair, and then a treadmill, and then a hat stand, and then an emaciated teenager being measured by a doctor, and then a laundry basket. For each image, I note down my interest out of ten, finding nearly every one to be moderately interesting, in the six to seven range. A very attractive wardrobe gets an eight. Overweight woman in a leotard? Six. Set of dumbbells? Five. Sporadically the tone blares in my ears. I am painfully aware that I am blinking far more throughout this test than I would if I didn't have sensors stuck to my face.

I cannot have any peace of mind if I treat
other people unfairly.   1 2 3 4 5

People tell me how they really feel.   1 2 3 4 5

I sometimes feel a spiritual connection to
others that I can't explain.   1 2 3 4 5

I like it when people can do whatever they
want without strict rules.   1 2 3 4 5

When I fail at something, I become more
determined to do a good job.   1 2 3 4 5

I worry more than others that something
will go wrong in the future.   1 2 3 4 5

Other people control me too much.   1 2 3 4 5

I am usually able to get other people to
believe me, even when I know that what
I am saying is exaggerated or untrue.   1 2 3 4 5

Circumstances often force me to do things
against my will.   1 2 3 4 5

I know what I want to do in my life.   1 2 3 4 5

By the time I come back to the silhouette questions again, several hours have passed and I am dizzy. Danielle has given me the same printouts, the same questions. I have to answer them afresh, except that this time my head is fuzzy and the little black figures are dancing on the paper. I rub residual glue from the sensors away from the skin under my eye. I frown. I concentrate.

Please mark the silhouette that best represents your body shape. Please mark how you wish to look. Which is the most attractive silhouette? Which is the most attractive silhouette to the opposite sex?

There is no need to overthink this, I tell myself. Just pick one of the pictures. It doesn't matter. I am the subject, not the critic, and all I have to do is be. It is someone else's Ph.D.; it is someone else's work to study me. I am her Mrs Gaskell.

And still, as the little bodies swim across the page, my mind wanders to my own work, to the desk in the Rare Books Reading Room where, on any other weekday, I would be sitting with a stack of dusty books. How much easier it would be, I think, if the subjects of my thesis were available to come down to my lab and answer a few questions.

Please mark the silhouette that best represents your body shape, Mrs Gaskell. Please mark how you wish to look. Which is the most attractive silhouette to the opposite sex, Mrs Gaskell? What do you think Mr Norton wishes to see, when, in his mind, he unwraps you from your shawls and unbuttons your dress and unhooks your stays and lifts up your chemise? Which of these silhouettes would he see, then, in his mind's eye?

I am known as an 'eager beaver' because of my enthusiasm for work.	1 2 3 4 5
If I am embarrassed or humiliated, I get over it very quickly.	1 2 3 4 5
I find sad songs and movies boring.	1 2 3 4 5
I usually enjoy being mean to anyone who has been mean to me.	1 2 3 4 5
Please circle the number one; this is a validity item.	1 2 3 4 5
I can easily do things others would consider dangerous.	1 2 3 4 5
I am in contact with a divine and wonderful spiritual power.	1 2 3 4 5
I have so many faults that I don't like myself very much.	1 2 3 4 5
I have had moments of great, overwhelming joy.	1 2 3 4 5

1857

Via Sant'Isidoro

First thing in the morning, you went to your window and looked down at the Via Sant'Isidoro, the narrow road with its steep stone steps and sharp edges. In the early light, shadows cut the street in two, half bright, half murky and asleep. The bells of the Franciscan church on the corner rang every day at seven, and you gazed out at the white chapel and the monks emerging from the monastery behind, heads bowed. They looked antlike from your room on the fourth floor, and you wanted to reach out and prod them, flick their lowered chins and say, 'Look up! Look where you are! Look where we are!' It was your second month in Rome, and still these mornings thrilled and surprised you: how bright the sun, how crisp and clean the air from your window perch.

Below, the servants were beginning to move around. A maid came into view, climbing the steps towards the house in twos, her arms full of flowers; behind her, whistling, a man walking an enormous grey dog, which loped after him and sniffed the doorstep of the house. A horse clattered past along the Via degli Artisti, pulling a cart loaded with jangling wine bottles and driven by a peasant in dusty country clothes. Its hooves sounded loud and crisp against the cobbles. There were always noises in Rome, musical and distinct, but somehow they never merged, as they did in Manchester, into the kind of cacophonous background din that made your head ache.

The sun was climbing and you began to feel impatient. You were happy simply to sit and watch; you could stare for hours at the lichen creeping up the walls and the stone carvings built into it that announced, so triumphantly, *SPQR*. But you were also restless, and you drummed your fingers on the window frame, tapping out soundlessly the arpeggios your daughters practised on the piano. You were waiting. You had come to expect from your Roman mornings not only this moment of joyful surveillance, but a meeting.

You were so happy that you were anxious, all the time, that your happiness would come to an end.

And then there he was, as he had been every morning since you met, as you should never have doubted he would be. Mr Norton, trotting neatly up the steps, a bunch of violets in one hand, his hat in the other. You watched as he arranged it on his head and glanced at his reflection in the window, patting down the lapels of his coat.

'Mr Norton!' you called down, and he looked up slowly, as though he had known you were watching all along.

He joined you every day for breakfast, which was a raucous, crowded affair on the Casa Cabrale loggia, overlooking the courtyard: Mr and Mrs Story, their daughter Edith and bumptious little son Waldo, your girls Meta and Marianne, Aubrey de Vere and his Catholic friend, Reverend General Dr Manning. There was Mr Fields, a British artist, and Mr Hamilton Wilde, an American painter. Mrs Beecher Stowe had joined for three days in a row, and had been severe to everyone and talked politics over her eggs. Several times, Miss Hosmer had bustled in at the last minute, telling other guests to 'budge up' unapologetically, and helping herself to coffee. Other people drifted in and out, all notable for some great talent or other – sculptors, poets, philosophers, critics – and all with something interesting and humorous to say. You were right there in the thick of it, with a witty reply to everything, but you saved your best for Mr Norton.

A fortnight into your acquaintance, he had arrived early and found you the only one awake, and you had sat together at the empty breakfast table while the servants set places and brought in dishes around you. Since then it had become an unofficial daily engagement for the two of you to spend this time together, a snatched half-hour before your friends and family arrived, hungry and busy and anxious to join in. After breakfast the days took hold of you, and you were dragged off to see the city's endless exhibition of art and ruins and churches, and Mr Norton was there with you, to point out the paintings he thought you might like, to offer some anecdote of Roman history that brought to life a heap of stones, to catch your eye over the heads of the others and grin at some unvoiced joke that only the two of you understood.

Mr Norton was still on the street, squinting up at you in your window, when the Story's man opened the door to let him in. You watched him step inside before leaving your vantage point. As you crossed the room, you caught sight of your reflection in the mirror, and paused. You turned your face from one side to the other, and wondered whether you looked as bright as you felt, as fresh as you felt. You were forty-six, about to have breakfast with a man seventeen years your junior, who made you feel twenty, twenty-five, thirty years younger than you were. You laughed to yourself, and blinked at your reflection, and then hurried on.

'Mrs Gaskell.' He stood up when you came into the room.

'You're late this morning, Mr Norton,' you said, pulling out your own chair and dropping into it. 'I was looking out for you and thinking my day would be quite put out if you didn't come for our morning coffee.' You had developed a habit of talking quickly and too much to him. You were scared of silence in his company, and filled it constantly. 'And then of course, there you were, and I shouldn't have worried after all.'

He nudged the bouquet of violets that were resting near his coffee cup towards you. 'I rely on our morning meetings for a moment's sanity, before the Roman hulla-balloo starts up.'

'I have so much I wanted to say to you,' you said. You picked up the violets and played with them, rubbing the velvety petals between your fingers. 'I was awake three times last night thinking of things I absolutely had to say to Mr Norton the minute he arrived. I have an idea for a new story, a sort of ghost story, about a strange encounter in Rome, and I would like to test it out on you. But first, before I forget, I need to talk to you about that painting we saw yesterday in the Palazzo Barberini—'

'The Guido?'

'Yes, the portrait of Beatrice Cenci. My mind keeps coming back to it, and I wanted to tell you – I've decided – it is the most miserable painting I think I've ever seen.'

A laugh erupted from Mr Norton, loud and delighted. 'Mrs Gaskell, it is considered a masterpiece.'

'A miserable masterpiece,' you said, 'but really I don't believe it is as good as everyone says, and—'

You heard a noise behind you and turned, thinking it would be a servant bringing in the breakfast things. But instead, you saw Meta, bleary-eyed and crumpled from sleep.

'Ma,' she said, midway through a yawn. 'What are you doing up? Hello, Mr Norton.' She flopped down in a chair and turned to him. 'Mama is always the last to come to breakfast at home.'

'In Rome I am quite the early bird,' you said, and then, glancing at the clock over the mantelpiece, 'and so are you, today, Meta. We weren't expecting anyone else for twenty minutes at least.'

Meta shrugged. 'Marianne kept me up half the night

with her fidgeting and sleep-talking, and then the sun woke me up by shining right in my eyes and I thought there's nothing for it except to get up and make the best of the day. Coffee,' she said. 'I need coffee.'

Mr Norton was smiling at Meta, but you wondered whether he, too, was feeling a pang for your lost half-hour. Then, from behind you, someone said, 'Oh, we're starting early today I see,' and Mr Story appeared, beaming, and after him toddled Waldo, who ran straight to you and began to babble earnestly and incomprehensibly in a childish jargon based loosely on English, with some Italian thrown in, and then Edith emerged talking about a dream she'd had, and Mr de Vere moped in, offering blessings, and the room, which had been yours and yours alone only moments ago, was suddenly full of bustle and bodies and competing voices.

Later, as the coffee was being poured, and Mr Story was outlining the proposed sightseeing plan for the day, and Waldo was howling because he wanted more *pane*, Mr Norton leant across to you and said, very quietly, 'You owe me a ghost story, Mrs Gaskell. I won't forget.'

2013

Shakespeare and Company

The library room at Shakespeare and Company is smaller than Shu's bedroom, full of books, and, as the workshop begins, full of people too. We sit, thighs touching, on benches that run around the shelf-lined walls; someone is at my feet on the floor, leaning her back against my shins. The workshop leader, a man somewhere between my age and Max's, sits self-consciously in the window seat, a foot hooked on the ledge so that his knee is high enough for him to drape an arm across it. He looks as though he is posing for a portrait, as though, in his head, he is picturesque, iconic, like Hemingway and Fitzgerald and all his writer-predecessors in the city who made this bookshop famous. Behind him is the road, and beyond it, the river. Looming over the water is Notre-Dame, floodlit.

I gaze awkwardly around the room. I have spent so much time, recently, envious of Mrs Gaskell and her troupe of expatriate artists in Rome; so here I am, trying to embrace the idea that in this room at Shakespeare and Co. we are maintaining an important and cherished tradition of writers working side by side in Paris. I try to convince myself that the evening ahead is going to be as illuminating and provocative and thrilling as a salon at Gertrude Stein's. To my left is an American lady, talking to a lanky college-aged boy about a woman named Angela who may or may not be willing to emcee a poetry slam. On my other side, a young man is staring silently at a sheaf of papers in his hands. I read them over his shoulder: on the first is a poem titled 'The Maiden or the Mistress? A Riddle'. Max is sitting across the room, looking earnest and excited, occasionally catching my eye. I make a face at him that expresses, I hope, a combination of nerves, amusement and thrill.

'Welcome to the Writers' Workshop at Shakespeare and Company,' says the man in the window seat. 'For those who don't know already, I'm David. I'm a novelist. Hi.'

'Hi, David,' everyone mutters.

'I see some new faces tonight, so let's just go around the group and say who we are – just a name and where you're from, and whether you've brought anything for us to read.'

There is an agitated rustling in the room as, one by one, people introduce themselves. When Max says, 'Max,' and raises a hand in an awkward wave, I feel a sudden urge to laugh, and look down at the head of the person sitting between my feet. There are college students on their semesters abroad, British retirees, a man who spends his summers working on Alaskan oil rigs and his winters here, writing poetry. The American lady beside me is Christina from Texas, and she has brought some poems; the boy she was speaking to is Brad from California, who has a short story to share. The man with the 'Maiden or the Mistress' poem says his name is Jason and that he is from Birmingham, and then he waves his papers and mutters that he's brought 'a verse of sorts'.

'Nell,' I say. 'From London. I brought,' I pause, and wonder if this is really such a good idea, 'some non-fiction.' I have printed out fifteen copies of a passage I've written about William Wetmore Story and the salons he held at his house in Rome every Friday.

When we have been around everyone, there is a silence while David scrutinizes his register.

'All right,' he says. 'Let's start. Christina – shall we hear from you?'

Nobody has brought enough copies, so we huddle around scraps of paper, three or four to a sheet. First, someone who is not the author reads the work aloud. Then a second person, also not the author, reads it aloud. Then, the author reads it aloud. After that, there is a free-for-all of criticism that begins politely and then gradually, timidly, edges towards negativity.

In this way, we make it through Christina's poems ('Has the author really earned the expletives in the final stanza?'), Brad's short story about a suicidal Iraq veteran ('Too much exposition'; protagonist 'unrelatable') and a series of haiku by an English girl called Millie, which, the group agreed, were pithy but, ultimately, hackneyed. I have said nothing, so far, and have been keeping my eyes fixed on the words on the page to avoid being invited to contribute. Max has, occasionally, chipped in with encouragement and reading suggestions. 'Your story reminds me a bit of "A Perfect Day for Bananafish" by Salinger,' he tells Brad. 'Have you read it?' Brad says he has not read 'A Perfect Day for Bananafish'.

'All right,' says David, again, and I brace myself to hear my own name called. But: 'Jason. Let's have a look at that "verse of sorts".'

Beside me, Jason twists on the bench and passes out sheets of paper as though being forced to do so against his will. There are even fewer copies of Jason's work than of the previous offerings, and they run out about half-way around the room. With nothing to read, I make do, instead, with watching other people as they scan the pages. Max has shifted so that he can see someone else's copy: his eyes widen, and then flick towards me. I can't quite read his expression, beyond suggesting a degree of alarm.

I mouth: 'What?' across the room to him, but he just widens his eyes again.

Christina volunteers to be the first reader, and there is a brief commotion while a copy of the poem is given up from the other side of the room and passed to her. Then, she begins.

'The Maiden or the Mistress,' she reads, in a cheerful, slightly nasal voice. 'A Riddle.' She clears her throat. 'With her angelic eyes, she blesses me with grace. I want to touch her body and her skin and her fair face.'

I relax. This is, clearly, not the literary highlight of the evening. Nor is it, though, the worst thing that has been read aloud so far: some of Millie's haiku were in a similar vein. Christina reads on. We hear about the woman's skin ('snow-white') and her hair ('which waves like an ocean'). Then, the poem broadens its preoccupation to a discussion of women in general: 'Womankind is fickle; in her temper she is cruel. In not-so-distant centuries she faced the ducking stool.'

I laugh, and then look around and realize that nobody knows if this is supposed to be funny. Two of the American college girls appear horrified. I don't dare look at Max. Christina herself fidgets awkwardly on the bench as she goes on to read several couplets examining the misleading nature of feminine beauty and the impossibility of ensuring a woman's fidelity. 'Behind her sweet demeanour and her diamond eyes, she hides her lasciviousness and her lies.' Beside me, Jason is tense. He is jiggling his foot on the floor, his thigh vibrating against mine. I edge away, closer to Christina, to break the connection.

'I try to find her meaning, opening her up like drawers. But the truth is that the maiden and the mistress are both whores.'

Christina lets the page fall into her lap. The poem is over. I take the opportunity to read it for myself. The end-of-line rhymes stand out down the page: cruel, stool; play, betray; eye, sly; make, forsake; and so on until the triumph of 'drawers, whores'. I focus on them until I feel certain I won't laugh, and then I risk glancing at Max: he is sitting very still, his face giving nothing away.

'Right,' says David, 'who wants to read for the second time?'

There is a dead silence in the room. As it unfolds, I become aware first of the sound of traffic passing on the road outside, and then the creaking of floorboards all around us as, in other parts of the shop, customers buy books.

Since beginning my Ph.D., I have become a connoisseur of the awkward silence. I know its variations, its moods, and its outcomes.

In the doctoral seminar, we ride them out timorously, shame-facedly, after each presentation; nobody wants to be the one to ask the first question. This is an optimistic, teeth-gritted kind of silence: we know it will be broken and, more often than not, we know who will break it, because the doorsteps-in-Dickens girl has developed a reputation for being confident and remarkably persistent in her focus on 'doorsteps' in every literary genre, in every period of history. After seconds that feel, in that bated-breath quiet, like minutes, her voice will ring out like a school bell announcing the end of a lesson, and everybody relaxes.

In my one-on-one meetings with Joyce, the awkward silence has a different, more acute quality. 'Have you considered the influence of Swedenborg on Elizabeth Barrett Browning?' she will say. 'Do you think Walter Benjamin's analysis of the aura of the artwork and mechanical reproduction is relevant to Harriet Hosmer's neoclassical project?' And I will sit and stare at my fingers gripping my pen, and at the page they are resting on, and at the words I have scribbled on the paper. I will implore my own brain to think, to say something smart, or just to say anything, and meanwhile the silence will settle over the room like weather. I feel it on my skin, clogging my pores and clouding my thoughts.

And yet, for all my recent experience, the awkward silence of the Shakespeare and Company workshop after the first reading of Jason's poem is striking: it is gloriously, agonizingly, stomach-churningly long. It takes on a sort of form in the room, a giant squatting amongst us, and all around it is the flickering and darting of the eyes of workshop participants, staring at each other, and down at the floor, and out of the window behind David's head.

'I'll just read it myself,' Jason says, and David looks so relieved to hear a human voice that he seems prepared to overlook the break with protocol.

When Jason has finished, there is a beat that threatens to swell into the silence we suffered before. Then: 'I thought the rhymes were really good,' Millie says, cautiously.

'I liked how, at the beginning, you gave a description of the appearance of the woman,' says Brad. 'You really painted a picture of what she looked like.'

'I thought the language you used was really classic. Like a Shakespeare poem,' says one of the British retirees.

There is a lull and everyone looks tense until an elderly Englishman says, 'I agree with Millie that the rhyme scheme is effective.'

I wonder whether I, too, should speak to the effectiveness of the rhymes.

'The thing is,' says one of the American college girls, in a tone of voice that immediately makes me sit up a little straighter, 'it's just super-offensive. It's like, totally sexist.'

'It's like,' her friend says, 'what century am I in? Hello? Did I fall asleep and wake up in 1950?'

'Or, like, *1850*?' says the first girl.

Christina sighs loudly, as though she has been holding her breath for a long time, and then says, 'Honestly, I'm glad y'all have brought that up. I found it hard to read. It's just really . . . it's very negative and I personally found it distasteful.'

'Yeah,' says a man in a Breton-stripe top, with an ambiguous accent, 'it seems like fairly standard-issue misogyny.'

Suddenly everyone has something to contribute, and David has to speak over several other comments when he says, half-shouting, 'Let's take some time to remember that the *speaker* of the poem is separate from the *author* of the poem.'

'Maybe,' says Max, 'if this poem is written in the voice of a misogynist, Jason could really dramatize that, to show that he, as the poet, is in control of the narrative.'

Max's contribution seems to have calmed the room somewhat, and for the first time, I feel as though I have something to offer. I say, 'Have you read Robert Browning's "Porphyria's Lover", Jason?'

Jason ignores me. 'You don't get it at all,' he says. 'I'm writing from my personal experience of women. I'm writing about my experiences.'

'Wow,' says Christina, 'just wow.' She crosses her arms, which has the effect of shunting me back towards Jason.

I squeeze my legs together and try to make myself as small as possible.

'You have all misread my work,' Jason says. 'You're letting your personal prejudices obstruct your appreciation of literature.'

'What personal prejudice is that?' says the Breton-top man. 'That women are human beings?'

'This is bullshit.'

'You should be ashamed of yourself.'

The volume in the room is growing and growing until Christina says, not loudly but so shrilly that it cuts through the noise: 'This is not how it was in the days of Hemingway and Fitzgerald! This is not how they would have done it!'

'If it helps,' says Max, 'it's not the real Shakespeare and Company.'

The workshop is over, and we are crossing the river on our way back to Shu's apartment. He is holding my hand very tightly. I am feeling exhausted, deflated: in the moment, I thought the workshop was funny, found the characters around me and the squabbles entertaining; but now, back in the real world, it all strikes me as unbearably sad.

I think about the Paris of Gertrude Stein – Picasso and Djuna Barnes and Matisse and Jean Rhys and all the others, walking the same streets at the same time – and shake my head. 'No,' I say. 'It's not the real Shakespeare and Company.'

'No, I mean, literally,' Max says. 'It's literally not the real one. It's a different location, different owner. They just named it after the original Shakespeare and Co., in the sixties, I think. It's just a . . . an *hommage*. A replica after the fact.'

We walk through a cloud of cigarette smoke, drifting up from the ashtray of a table outside a bistro.

'It's so sad to think of all these people coming to Paris to be part of something that doesn't exist any more,' I say.

By now all the workshop participants will have dispersed around the city, to their Airbnb rentals and their garrets, to their laptops and their malfunctioning printers which will fail again, next week, to produce enough copies for everyone in the library room at Shakespeare and Company. Some of them will be writing again already, tapping away at their keyboards, and Jason will be smoking and looking sourly out of the window and thinking about how feminists have ruined art, and David will be sitting with his friends, or his girlfriend, saying he's not sure he can carry on leading that workshop, man, those people get crazier by the week, and it's disrupting his own creative process.

'It doesn't have to be sad,' says Max. 'People still find each other here. People still make new things. We're here, aren't we?'

His hand is solid and hot in mine, as we turn onto Rue d'Aboukir, past the taxidermist's window display of winged mice.

Mr Charles Eliot Norton's Guide to Rome and its Environs

The Colosseum at Sunset

It was a plan that kept being put off: first Mr Story was ill, and then Mr Norton, and then on the third attempt, you were all ready to go when one of Marianne's head-aches set in, and as the end of your time in Rome drew closer, you began to think it would never happen, this trip to the Colosseum at night. But it was truly worth it, Mr Norton said, to see how the stone arches threw shadows, lengthening first as the sun dropped lower and lower, how they crystallized in the moonlight. You could really feel, then, he said, the ghosts of Christian martyrs in the arena, could almost hear the roar of the old Roman crowds.

On your penultimate night in the city, the plan finally came together. You set off, bundled up in shawls and scarves. It was nearly summer, but the air was cold that evening, and the Storys insisted that the Colosseum was a sickly, deathly place. Their daughter, Edith, had almost died years ago after her first visit to see it. In the carriage on the way, you fussed over Meta and Marianne, and Mr Norton fussed over you, and wondered whether you should all go back for more layers. But as you drew up beside the ruins, you forgot about the cold and looked instead at the stone, gold in the last of the light, and Mr Norton said, 'Yes, like this. This is the way to see it.'

Inside the Colosseum, it was still. You couldn't hear the clatter of carriages and horses' hooves still passing on the road outside. You couldn't hear church bells ringing. Wind blew over the broken walls and picked up the leaves and tendrils of creepers clinging to the stone. There was another group of visitors at the far end of the arena, but they were far away enough that they seemed less like people than the spectres Mr Norton had promised you'd meet.

You watched your daughters weave amongst the rubble of the amphitheatre, and, later, their faces illuminated in torchlight as darkness fell. And it was then, as you were sitting surveying it all – their wondering, delighted expressions, the play of the flames against the ruins – that Mr Norton placed himself beside you and said, 'Now is the time, Mrs Gaskell, for your ghost story.' The auditorium was waiting, its empty seats hungry for occupants, its gigantic floor and underground passages poised to support a performance.

'Absolutely not,' you said. 'It's chilling enough, my tale, in the brightest daylight.'

The Campagna

The next morning, you hired a carriage to take you out. Meta and Marianne stayed at home to oversee packing, and you went with Mr Norton and Mr Field and Miss Hosmer, out beyond the city walls to the strange, undulating countryside beyond. There was an odd silence to the Campagna, even when the wind rolled over it, even when Mr Norton pointed out that the mounds in the land were not hillocks in the English sense, but bulges of ruins pushing up through the ground. He told the driver to stop the carriage and climbed down to show you: he dug a heel roughly into the grass, and turned up a fragment of pottery. When he did it again, he found a coin, glinting in the earth, and when he rubbed the dirt away and held it up for you to see, you read the name 'CAESAR' stamped on its side. The Campagna was a treasure chest.

'My story,' you said, as the carriage rolled on, 'is about a young English bride. After her wedding she was tormented by a recurring dream. She would wake her new husband every night, crying out in her sleep. No matter what she did, no matter what medicine she took, she dreamt the same dream night after night, and it so frayed her nerves that she became exhausted and infirm.'

'What was the dream?' asked Mr Norton.

'It was a dream,' you said, 'about a face.'

The Palazzo Barberini and the Studio of William Wetmore Story

'The bride's husband took her to every doctor he could find,' you said. 'She tried sea bathing, and abstaining from tea, and bed rest, but nothing worked. Still, in her dreams, the face visited her and made her terrified. In the end, the husband decided, there was nothing left but to take her abroad, and see whether European air might cure her of her vision. He took her first to Paris, where she showed some small signs of improvement. A French doctor wrote the husband a letter of introduction to a medical man at Rome who was skilled in the healing of nervous disorders, and with this in hand, the couple set off for Italy.'

The carriage had dropped you at the Palazzo Barberini, where you went to look one more time at Guido's portrait of Beatrice Cenci: the girl's red eyes stared hollowly out of the canvas and you insisted, again, that you thought it was depressing: more depressing than ever today, you thought, because tomorrow you were leaving and would never see it again. Mr Norton suggested that you visit Mr Story at work, 'to see some real, living art in the making'. There was a grin on his face as he said this that made you wonder whether, perhaps, Mr Norton was as sceptical of Mr Story's 'real, living art' as you were of the maudlin, morbid face of Beatrice Cenci.

Together, with Mr Field and Miss Hosmer in tow, you left the cool air of the palazzo and waited a moment by the fountain for your eyes to adjust to the daylight. Gradually, the stones and creepers of the courtyard became dark and visible again.

'And so,' you continued, as you turned the corner onto the narrow little Via di San Nicola da Tolentino, 'the husband brought his afflicted wife to Rome.'

Mr Norton pointed out the doorway that led to the studio, and held it open for you. You stepped inside.

Mr Story was at work on a clay model when you came into the main room, and for a while he pretended not to notice you were there. You hovered nearby, watching him frown and slide his hands over the head and shoulders of a glowering, hunched woman, and pinch her brows into a more profound glare. He hummed as he worked, a song you recognized from the *pifferari*'s playing on the Corso.

'It's Cleopatra,' Mr Norton told you, and on hearing his voice, Mr Story looked up and beamed.

'Friends!' he said. 'How long have you been standing there? I was so absorbed, I had no idea I had an audience!'

You wandered between statues: Venus, naked, half-covering herself with limp hands; Medea, clutching a dagger, deep in thought. Mr Story pointed out the intricacies of the drapery, the historical accuracy of the costumes, the facial expressions that, he insisted, portrayed the spiritual life of his subjects.

'You see, here,' he said, gesturing at an amulet on the marble wrist of a large, squat woman, 'it is these details, my dear friends, that have earned me my reputation as, not only a sculptor, but a poet too. My marble speaks a kind of poetry, people say.'

'Very good, Mr Story,' Mr Norton said. 'Masterful. Yes. Poetic. The drapery is exquisitely done.'

'For a while,' you said, turning away, and talking loud enough that only Mr Norton could hear, 'the wife felt better. The dreams stopped and she felt, finally, that she could breathe again. The Italian air seemed to be working. Rome had cured her of her dream.'

The Pantheon

It started to rain while you were inside, and the hole in the domed roof let down a curtain of droplets that splashed against the marble floor. You stood beneath it and felt the water on your face, the strangest feeling, to be rained on indoors, as though the weather had followed you in.

After lunch, you had exchanged Mr Field and Miss Hosmer for Marianne and Meta, who had finished packing and wanted to visit the Pantheon: somehow, after three months in Rome, you had never been. This was your last chance. You watched your girls moving around the edges of the space, inspecting statues and reading aloud from their *Murray's Guide*: '. . . the burial place of Raphael . . . The circular hall is one hundred and forty-two feet in diameter, exclusive of the walls . . .' Mr Norton, after helping them find their way to Raphael's tomb, behind the third chapel on the left-hand side, crossed the floor and stood beside you in the pillar of rain.

'Where were we?' you asked.

'Rome had cured her of her dream,' he said.

'It had,' you said, at once. 'The bride was so much improved in Rome that at first the husband thought there was no need to visit the expert to whom they had been given a note of introduction. But as the end of their visit drew near, he decided to call upon the doctor and invite him to examine the bride, to be sure she was strong enough to go home. After extending the invitation, the husband returned to his hotel with the doctor, a handsome man with great, dark eyes and white hair. The wife came to the door of their suite to greet them, but on seeing the doctor's face, she turned pale and fell down in a faint.'

'It was the face from her dream?' asked Mr Norton.

'It was the face from her dream,' you said, savouring the words.

The Catacombs of St Calixtus

Why would you not, on your final night in the city, go to the Catacombs? You had been all over Rome that day, but there was a panicky, urgent feeling building in your chest that stopped you feeling tired: time was running out, and there was more to see, more to say.

There were many steps down, and with each one you felt a little colder. The air around you was changing, shrinking, as you descended into the dark. You could feel Marianne behind you, and see Meta ahead, but the light from the torches was flickering and unstable, and for a moment it all seemed unreal, two-dimensional, like a painting, until you heard Mr Norton's voice up ahead, 'Can you see, here, the engravings of the early Christian martyrs in the rock?'

The ground was wet underfoot as you padded through dark passages, between spaces cut into the rock. When you moved your light over it, you saw the white glow of human bone, lying in dirt centuries old. You waited for revulsion to set in, but looking on the hollow ribcages, the scattered clavicles, the skulls that sat emptily amid nests of dust, you felt only burning curiosity about these long-gone humans, who looked so vague now, and would once have been specific. Perhaps they, too, had wished for more time.

When you emerged back into the evening air, breathless after the climb, you turned to Mr Norton and in a rush told him the rest of the story.

'That night, the husband left his wife to rest while he went to dinner, and when he returned to their rooms he found she had vanished. He ran down and began to ask the hotel staff and people in the dining rooms whether they had seen his wife, where she had gone. He sent his maid, his manservant, the hotel porters out into the streets to search for her. They came back all telling the same tale: that there were reports all around the city of sightings of a young Englishwoman being driven away in a carriage in the company of the handsome Roman doctor. They had passed the city walls, and vanished into the Campagna. And she was never seen again.'

Spithöver's English Bookshop, 85 Piazza di Spagna

On the morning of your departure, you went to the English Bookshop in the Piazza di Spagna on the pretence of wanting to buy photographs of monuments to take home for Mr Gaskell. Mr Norton had told you that

Spithöver's was the best place for souvenirs, and so you asked him to take you there.

You went early, right after breakfast, and the artist's models were still crowded on the Spanish Steps in clusters, waiting for painters to hire them. A group of women stood together, all dressed as Mary Magdalene and holding grief-stricken, mournful poses. Higher up was a gathering of scheming Judas Iscariots. Their shadows slithered down the steps below them. A few shabbily dressed, paint-stained young men paced around between the groups, eyeing the postures and calling out to ask the models' rates.

Spithöver's was dark inside, and it took a moment for your eyes to make out the rows of Murray's guides and copies of Byron and *Corinne* lining the shelves.

'Here,' said Mr Norton, presenting you with a bound collection of photographs. 'This has all the significant sights – the Colosseum, the Forum. And, in addition, a copy of your favourite Guido portrait.'

You were distracted and didn't smile. 'Yes,' you said. 'Maybe.' And then you saw it, bright and new, freshly stocked, your own name shining on the spine: *The Life of Charlotte Brontë* by Mrs. Gaskell, Vol. 1, *The Life of Charlotte Brontë* by Mrs. Gaskell, Vol. 2. It gave you a thrill to see – half pleasure, half anxiety – and you reached to take the two volumes down, one after the other.

'What's that?' asked Mr Norton.

You handed it to him. 'A gift,' you said. 'For when you miss my ghost stories.'

In a few hours, you would commence the reverse of

the journey you had made only three months earlier, but which seemed to have happened to a different person altogether, a different Mrs Gaskell. Soon you would be in Marseille, and then in Paris, and then in Calais, and then in London, and then – your stomach tightened – in Manchester, in the house on Plymouth Grove, and the bed you shared with Mr Gaskell. You would be returned to that old life, the one that had been yours when you wrote the book that was, now, open in the palm of Mr Norton.

He read the title page with a broad smile, then closed and stroked the cover as though it were a small animal in his hands.

'I hope you know that I plan to give myself very little opportunity to miss you, Mrs Gaskell.'

'You'll come to Manchester?'

'As soon as I can.'

You nodded. 'Yes. Good.'

It was quiet in the bookshop. Mr Spithöver was nowhere to be seen. You looked around half-heartedly for someone to take your money for the book, but were relieved when nobody came. The longer it took, the longer you could spend in the hushed sanctuary of the shop, away from the bustle at the Casa Cabrale and the panicked requests of your daughters for last-minute visits or purchases, from the reality of the matter: that you were leaving. That tomorrow there would be no coffee with Mr Norton on the loggia, nor the day after that, nor the day after that.

'It breaks my heart to leave Rome.'

'I will see you again soon,' he said. 'I promise. I promise.'

Part Two

SALIVA STUDY

2015

Procrastination: Three Techniques

One: Become Lucky

The Internet is a catalogue of unlikely opportunity. I am in the habit, now, a year and a half into my Ph.D., of sitting in the Rare Books Reading Room, surrounded by journals and volumes and tomes I am not reading, and instead, entering competitions online. The best sites for this are the women's magazines – *Vogue, Elle, Glamour* – who tantalize with the possibilities of luxury: bright, glossy pictures of happy, skinny people. The web pages feature airbrushed models holding up handbags or make-up, wearing expensive clothes, and below the photographs, a simple form. *Enter your email address for a chance to win.* I have become expert at answering questions constructed by PR teams to force the internalization of marketing messages. *Where did such-and-such a designer look for inspiration for her new collection? A – Philadelphia, B – Texas, C – Barcelona?* Give me free holidays. New wardrobes. Phones. Two tickets to see a show and an overnight stay in a five-star hotel.

The word count of my thesis has not budged in weeks. It is visible at the bottom of a document that sticks out beneath the Internet browser: a real, ignorable fact. Better, surely, to live in the realm of the imaginary, to think that perhaps good things will be given to me for free, that I will not have to work for it, because I've tried working, really truly I have, and it hasn't worked at all.

It is the second semester of my second year at King's. I have spent a year and five months purportedly researching the expatriate artistic community in mid-to-late-nineteenth-century Rome, and I have never felt less interested, or less inspired. My days have become grindingly repetitive: the commute from home to the library, the same librarians behind the Issue and Returns desk, the same people with the same annoying coughs and sniffs and tics all around me in the reading room, the same over-priced coffee from the second-floor cafe.

Two: Time Travel

I daydream about the future and the past in equal measure. I think about last summer, which I spent with Max in Boston. I taught a class at BU, which paid for the flight from London and provided an excuse I could give to Joyce about why I'd be unavailable for supervision for three whole months. In the afternoons, when my classes were over and the students had dispersed, Max and I would work on our writing in air-conditioned cafes, and in the evenings we'd cook, we'd see movies, we'd do the things that normal couples do when they live in the same country, the same city. We went out to eat a lot at Lineage, the restaurant where we'd had our first, awkward non-date;

we had a favourite table there, and always ordered fish tacos. At the end of each working week, Max would collect me from campus in his little grey car, and we'd drive south to his family's cottage by the beach on Cape Cod. It was the longest we had ever spent in each other's company, an uninterrupted stretch of summer. I had worried beforehand that we might struggle to live together after being apart for so long, but I couldn't get tired of him. I was endlessly delighted: by his body, his voice, the way he thought and moved and said, 'I love you,' all the time, as though it was a form of punctuation. We ate lobster rolls and lay on the sand and listened to the waves and said to each other, over and over, differing versions of: *this is the life we want; this; just this; just you and me and whatever else comes our way.*

But I was becoming frantic, even then, about the future: once Max left Paris, we had begun a transatlantic affair that exhausted us both. I applied for conferences, scholarships, anything that would pay for me to get to America. He scrimped and saved, doing odd jobs and painting houses, to afford the flights to London. Then I started teaching undergraduate classes at King's, and couldn't visit him; and then he started teaching undergraduate classes at BU, and couldn't visit me. The daily Skype calls we had begun while he was in France became an inconvenience: the five-hour time difference meant that it was either too early for him, interrupting his working day, or too late for me, keeping me up. And so, while I was in Boston over the summer, I was full of schemes and plans to ensure that our separation wouldn't be indefinite, that there was an end in sight.

I would finish my Ph.D. by the middle of 2016. I would be free, then, to move to Boston, and we could start our life there, together, really together. We sat on the porch of the beach cottage, looking out at the ocean, and my heart thudded in my chest as I set out this timeline to Max and said, 'There's just one thing, though.'

'What's that?'

'If I come to Boston, if I'm going to *move* to Boston, permanently, I'd need, you know, a green card.'

'Yes, sure.'

The cottage on Cape Cod had belonged to Max's family for several decades: inside, it was an archive of old black-and-white photos of his grandparents and great-grandparents, of marriage certificates, domestic paraphernalia, artefacts left behind by generation after generation of this American family around whose edges I was hovering.

I swallowed. 'So that would mean, you know, that we'd have to get married.'

I couldn't look at him as I said this. I covered my face with my hands and squeezed my eyes shut. Then I felt him reaching out and peeling my fingers back. I squinted up at him. His expression was confused, and I thought, *I've freaked him out, I've been too pushy.*

'I thought,' he said, and then stopped. 'I thought that was obvious. I thought that was already the plan.'

'It was?' I said, and he said, again, that yes, of course,

he'd always thought we would get married when I finished my Ph.D. The casualness with which he says this, the look of bemusement on his face at my anxiety, astonishes and delights me. This momentous thing is obvious to him, a given: we will spend our lives together.

And so, when I am not reminiscing about the summer, I am fantasizing about the future. This is a life I was never before sure would be mine: gold band encircling my ring finger. Things that were never interesting to me begin to hold a strange, relevant fascination: I notice when my old classmates from school post pictures online of themselves in white dresses, clutching bouquets; I scrutinize the photographs. A leaflet posted on a noticeboard in a cafe near my house, advertising a nearby stately home as a wedding venue, which previously I would not even have stopped to read, I now ponder. I imagine what it would be like to get married there, to be the sort of person who gets married in a stately home.

I am going to marry Max. That thing that other people do – where they get dressed up and say they love each other in front of their family and friends – I am going to do that with Max. After that, we will have children, because that is what always happens next, and what I have always assumed I will do, and what, I am realizing now, I want to do. He and I will move into a house in Boston or London or LA or Paris and create more people to live in it with us. I imagine them, too: our future progeny, pink and scrunched, his nose, my eyes, the best of each of us. It is fascinating and delightful to me, the thought that this can be mine, that I will participate in the same series

119

of pre-ordered choices as everyone else, and be happy doing so. I am going to marry Max, and I am going to become a mother.

At the end of the summer, when I was about to leave Boston and was standing in the international departures terminal at Logan Airport gasping with tears and desperate to delay the moment I had to walk through security and away from Max, a TSA agent came up to us.

'Who's leaving?' he asked.

Sniffing, I raised a hand and said, 'Me.'

'You're not gonna see each other for how long?'

'I don't know!' I wailed, and Max said, 'A few months, probably.'

'Where you from?' he asked me.

I said, 'London,' through tears, as though it was the most tragic place anyone could possibly live.

The agent nodded sympathetically and told Max he could go back to the check-in desk and ask for a security pass, which would mean he could come with me to the gate. 'You can put her right on the plane,' the agent said. Max was willing to do it, but I shook my head and wiped my eyes, suddenly embarrassed about crying and making a fuss.

The agent frowned, shrugged and turned to Max. 'Next time, you better put a ring on it, my friend.'

'I will,' Max said, sounding apologetic. 'I really will.'

On the other side of the security check, I saw the same agent again, who gave me a nod of recognition, a thumbs-up, and then pointed at his ring finger enthusiastically.

Three: Consider alternative paths

Perhaps, after all, this Ph.D. is not worth my while. I think back to that day in the Louvre when Max had told me to write about what moved me. It had felt like a break-through. But when I gaze at my surroundings in the Rare Books Reading Room, that clarity of purpose dims. The world inhabited by my subjects still seems bright and seductive, and the subjects themselves – the Brownings and Harriet Hosmer and William Story and, above all, Mrs Gaskell – are still alive to me. The more I know of them, the more I love them. But I couldn't be further from them, here at my desk in the British Library. My solitary student life could not be more different to the Roman days they spent together, creating, collaborating, loving each other.

My research is laborious and unrewarding: I am claw-ing at an enormous cliff face, hoping to tunnel through it, but the rock is unbreakable. My *Anglistica & Americana* book is ragged with re-reading; I know sections of the letters by heart. But the more familiar I become with my subjects and their work, the less certain I am that I have anything of academic value to say. The enormity of the task ahead – writing 100,000 words of pure, never-known-before knowledge – is off-putting, impossible, preferably avoidable.

I look up jobs all the time: colleges in Massachusetts that need writing tutors, arts charities that need coordin-ators, anything, really, that would offer a good enough excuse to walk away from my research in London and run, instead, to a new life with Max in Boston. In less despairing moments I go back to applying for Ph.D.-related events in the US. I am not fussy about where. I apply for conferences in New York, workshops in LA, a research fellowship in Texas. Anywhere there would be nearer to Max than here.

I am tired of being alone all the time, of conversations on Skype in which we tell each other about our days in desperate and minute detail, just for the sake of having something to say. I want a real life, shared with a real human, not just a cipher on a screen.

It is through all my rigorous *applying* for things – jobs, fellowships, grants – that I get sucked into the world of online competitions. I am throwing my hat into so many rings that a few more seem entirely worthwhile. *Consider me*, I am saying to the universe, daily, hourly. *Pick me for a change, a transformation, a luxury spa weekend for two.*

1857

Hornets' Nest

The front door of the house at Plymouth Grove looked just how it had when you left, and yet, somehow, though you knew it couldn't be, darker. It was drizzling as the hackney carriage pulled up outside the house; perhaps it was the effect of damp on the wood panels that made it seem that way. You followed your daughters down the drive; they were running, skipping through the rain. It felt to you that you were moving through flood water, that whatever sense of duty and inevitability was propelling you forwards was fighting a weaker but frantic desire to turn around, to get back in the carriage and drive away. The front door opened. The girls ran through. You followed them, and even inside, as you shook off the bad weather and the journey's cramps in the hallway, the place seemed dim.

Marianne, at least, was happy to be home, and ran down to the kitchen to see her beloved maid, Hearn. Meta, you thought, must be feeling similar to you: she looked perplexed as she surveyed the familiar furniture of the parlour, and reached out an uncertain hand to touch the fabric of the drapes.

'Can you believe, Mama, it was only days ago we were in Rome?'

You could not, you said, and yet there was part of you that still, for all that, could not believe that you were *not* in Rome, could not believe that you were instead in Manchester, damp from the journey and listening to the bustle of the servants bringing in your things and seeing, there, in the doorway of his study, a man with a thick, greying beard and dim-eyed smile. You could not believe that that man was your husband.

'Welcome home,' said Mr Gaskell, and even in his deep, assured voice, the word 'home' sounded uncertain.

You had been good about writing to him at first. Your early weeks in Rome had been full of letters: you told him about the places you were visiting and the people you were meeting and the stories they were telling you. You had known that he expected this, but also enjoyed it, that though he was scared of travel himself, and suspicious of foreign foods in particular, he was curious too, about other places. But by your second month away it seemed there was simply not much left to say. You had told him about all the most important sites, and had described all your new friends, had sent little sketches of the Casa Cabrale breakfasts, of Miss Hosmer charging down the Corso on her horse, Mr Story chewing his pipe at his desk, Mr Browning talking to his little eight-year-old son Pen as though he was an adult, and Mrs Browning talking to the same child as though he was barely two. You had described paintings and statues and churches and the strange, wide landscape of the Campagna. What more was there to say?

Except that now, alone with your husband on your first night back, the gaps between your letters, and their absence altogether in the past few weeks, seemed to take the form of a thick silence in the bedroom. It was crushing, and awkward – it made the room feel too small – and you hoped he would say nothing about it, and talk instead about Manchester, and whatever had been happening at the Cross Street Chapel, about his parishioners perhaps. You had told him all you could tell him about Rome.

But of course, in his direct, predictable way, he said, instead, 'How was Rome?'

You took a slow breath. You mulled over responses. It could be 'wonderful', or 'fine'. It could be 'lovely, but tiresome after a while'. The parties, the company, the busy, bustling breakfasts – it was exhausting, really, wasn't it? You could try to formulate some sort of falsehood about being happy to have left. But you could say none of these things.

'How are you, William?'

He cleared his throat and looked away from you.

'There has been some business here, while you have been away,' he said. He sat, heavily, on the bed. 'Some business about your book. The Brontë book. I have tried to handle it in your absence. I have tried not to bother you with it. But now you are home so it's right you should know.'

You thought, then, of Spithöver's bookshop, of the shadowy shelves and the piazza gleaming through the windows, and the artist's models massing on the Spanish Steps. Your book had been there. You had held it yourself, and handed it to Mr Norton. It had been there, and yet all the attendant worry, which you had known, after all, was coming – you had sensed and feared it – had been oddly absent. It had been only the good, the lovely fact of the words on the page, that existed in Rome.

You braced yourself. 'What business?' you asked.

Mr Gaskell began to take off his boots. 'There are over a hundred letters waiting for you downstairs,' was all he said.

The newspapers were full of it. They were jubilant with viciousness. They laid it out over and over again: the allegations made by Mrs Gaskell in her *Life of Charlotte Brontë* regarding the irreputable behaviour of one Lady Scott with one Branwell Brontë, late brother of the late Charlotte Brontë. Articles lingered over the fury of Lady Scott upon reading the biography, reported that she had written to the solicitors of Mrs Gaskell and of her publisher, threatening legal action, and that she had insisted on the recall of all unsold copies of the book. This, you read, had taken place, and at the end of May, only two days ago, a letter from your solicitor had appeared in *The Times* and been reproduced in all the evening papers:

As solicitor for and on behalf of the Rev. W. Gaskell, and of Mrs. Gaskell his wife, the latter of whom is authoress of the *Life of Charlotte Brontë*, I am instructed to retract every statement contained in that work which imputes to a widowed lady, referred to, but not named therein, any breach of her conjugal, of her maternal, or of her social duties, and more especially of the statements contained in chapter 13 of the first volume, and chapter 2 of the second, which impute to the lady in question a guilty intercourse with the late Branwell Brontë. All those statements were made upon information believed to be well founded, but which, upon investigation, with the additional evidence furnished to me by you, I have ascertained not to be trustworthy. I am therefore authorized not only to retract the statements in question, but to express the deep regret of Mrs. Gaskell that she should have been led to make them.

The *Athenaeum*, to add insult to injury, had gone so far as to publish their own rebuke:

We are sorry to be called upon to return to Mrs. Gaskell's *Life of Charlotte Brontë*, but we must do so, since the book has gone forth with our recommendation. Praise, it is needless to point out, implied trust in the biographer as an accurate collector of facts. This, we regret to state, Mrs. Gaskell proves not to have been. It is in the interest of Letters that biographers should be deterred from rushing into print with mere impressions in place of proofs, however eager and sincere those impressions may be. They may be slanders, and as such they may sting cruelly. Meanwhile the *Life of Charlotte Brontë* must undergo modification ere it can be further circulated.

You were pale with rage. You stared at the headlines in the papers, at your name printed over and over, at the words that were put in your mouth by the lawyer, on the instruction of Mr Gaskell, and the way they had been thrown back at you. 'The deep regret of Mrs Gaskell'! You clutched the page so tightly it began to tear, and you had to force yourself to let it go, to return it to your desk. '. . . trust in the biographer as an accurate collector of facts. This, Mrs Gaskell proves not to have been.'

You stared at the window, and at the rain slamming against the glass. On the street, people were passing in carriages, the horses bending their heads into the wind. Your hands moved towards your correspondence paper and pen, and you didn't know, at first, who you were writing to, until the address somehow peeled itself from your pen onto the page: Mr C. E. Norton, Piazza di Spagna, Rome.

'Dear Mr Norton,' you wrote. 'I am back in the hornets' nest with a vengeance.'

2015

Loon Mountain

Max's face in the small box on the screen, eyebrows pinched together. Behind him is Boston. It is snowing. It has been snowing all winter, and now it is February, and it is still snowing. This has become a thing we talk about.

'How's the snow?' I ask.

'Still going,' he says. 'They say there's more on the way. They're calling it a "snow emergency". There's a parking ban on the street. My brother lost his car in a drift.'

It snows every winter in Boston, of course, and at first I thought Max was making an uncharacteristic fuss about it, until I realized that it really is worse than usual, this year. There are segments on the British news showing Bostonians skiing down huge white piles that have been ploughed off the streets. The mayor has issued a warning against people jumping into drifts from second-floor windows: *I'm asking people to stop this nonsense now. This isn't Loon Mountain, this is the city of Boston, where we're trying to remove snow off of the street and it becomes very dangerous.*

'What did you do today?' I say, every day, and every day Max says, 'I shovelled.'

He shovels his own driveway, and his parents' driveway, and the driveways of the houses being renovated by the developer for whom he does odd jobs. It snows, even as he shovels, and so when he has reached the end of a driveway, he says, he might as well just go back to the beginning and start again.

We are irritable with each other. Once we have exhausted the topic of the weather, he asks me about my day, and I say, 'I went to the library, and then I went to the gym, and then I came home.' I glare at him. It is his fault, I can't help feeling, that my life is so boring and repetitive and mundane. It is his fault that my days never vary. It is his fault, because he is not here with me.

If he asks what I did at the library, I tell him that I have discovered nothing new about Mrs Gaskell, but that I am in the running to win a pair of limited edition trainers. Often he does not ask.

Sometime after he left Paris for Boston, Max began emailing me poems. The idea was that it would be a casual, simple record of the things he had read, and which he thought I might like: he sends the poems each night before he goes to sleep; I wake up to them. They are as regular and predictable a part of my day as the morning news on the radio, as the announcement at the library every evening at 7.45: *The building is about to close. Would you please return all borrowed items to the issue desk. The building is about to close.*

Max's 'Poem of the Day' messages are numbered, and soon they become, without him really meaning them to, a counter tallying up the length of our separation. He stops sending them when we are together, and then picks up where he left off when we are apart. Poem of the Day, 105; Poem of the Day, 200.

Most days, I send him something in return. He gives me 'Poet's Work' by Lorine Niedecker – *Grandfather / advised me: / Learn a trade // I learned / to sit at desk / and condense* – and I respond with 'Michaelangelo: To Giovanni Da Pistoia When the Author Was Painting the Vault of the Sistine Chapel' by Gail Mazur: *I am not in the right place – I am not a painter*. He sends Matthew Arnold's 'Dover Beach': *Ah, love, let us be true / To one another! for the world, which seems / To lie before us like a land of dreams / So various, so beautiful, so new, / Hath really neither joy, nor love, nor light, / Nor certitude, nor peace, nor help for pain*. I reply with 'The Nineteenth Century and After', by Yeats: *Though the great song return no more / There's keen delight in what we have: / The rattle of pebbles on the shore / Under the receding wave.*

These are indirect, abstract conversations. These are the things we do not say on Skype, or have our own words for. We wrestle and argue and flirt and compliment and get tangled up in quotations. We are ventriloquists' dummies, yapping at one another in other people's voices. On my twenty-ninth birthday, he sends me 'Something Amazing Just Happened' by Ted Berrigan, which is an account of a dream in which the poet wins a Guggenheim Foundation Grant for the purpose of giving his friend Jim 'the best possible birthday present'.

> We have arranged for you and Jim to spend a year
> in London, in a
> flat off of King's Row.

During the year,
At your leisure, you might send us from time to
time copies of your
London works.

It is a clear and aching fantasy; it hurts to read; it makes me cry. It is a dream, recounted in a poem, discovered in a book and sent, via email, to me. It is not our life.

On Max's birthday, I send him Christina Rossetti's 'A Birthday'.

Lately, 'Poem of the Day' has become 'Poems of the Day'. It seems that the briefer and harder and more strained our nightly conversation has been, the more poems I will wake up to in my inbox. There are now routinely so many that I stop reading them all. On the bus, on my way to the library, I glance at the titles, and read the first two or three, and then give up. I feel swamped and annoyed. *Just say what you mean*, I think, as I skim through them. *Stop making me decipher these things. Stop making me read between the many hundreds of lines you have scooped up on your side of the Atlantic and hurled over here while I was sleeping.*

'Time Long Past', by Percy Bysshe Shelley. 'Lyric VII, from *In Memoriam A.H.H.*', by Alfred, Lord Tennyson. 'How Soon Hath Time', by John Milton.

'It just keeps piling up,' Max says.

'What does?' I ask. 'The snow?'

And he does mean the snow, but he means, too, the other things.

'I need to figure out my life,' he says, when I needle him. 'I'm nearly forty and doing odd jobs. I need to figure it out.'

'Come to London,' I say. I say this, if not daily, then at least every other day. 'Come to London, live rent-free with me. You can write here. We'll find a way to make my Ph.D. stipend stretch. I have extra money from teaching now. You wouldn't have to work.'

He just shakes his head and says, 'I need to figure this out for myself. I don't want to scrounge off you.'

It makes me want to scream at him. 'You'd do the same for me,' I say, 'if it were the other way around. If you were the one stuck in situ doing the Ph.D. and I was the one doing the odd jobs. You'd let me live with you and you'd help me out with money and you'd be so furious with me if you knew I was miserable but refusing your help.'

'I know,' he says. 'I know.'

'Just get on a plane,' I say. 'Just come. We'll figure it out.'

And then, nine times out of ten, he reverts to talking about the snow.

This isn't Loon Mountain. This is the City of Boston.

—

'Just come,' I say. 'Come to London. Then we can talk. Really talk.'

'I will,' he says.

'When?'

'I don't know.'

'Nuit Blanche', by Amy Lowell. 'A Mind of Winter', by Martha Kapos. 'Snow', by Vidyan Ravinthiran: *What I'm saying is, this isn't the right kind of snow.*

And then, at last, he books a flight, and I realize that in some part of myself I have been holding my breath, for weeks, months even, and that now, finally, I can exhale.

He is coming. He will be here soon.

2015

Upgrade Examination

*As a research student at King's you are registered as an M.Phil.
student initially. To receive a Ph.D. you must transfer to Ph.D.
status by undergoing a formal review. We call this process the
Upgrade Examination. The key principle for upgrading is that
you are well on course to produce research of the required standard within the permitted timescale. The Upgrade Examination
must take place between 9 and 18 months after you begin your
course of study.*

'It's time,' says Joyce. 'It's time to upgrade.'

I groan. Joyce shrugs in a manner that reminds me of
my mother, the way she used to look at me when I was a
teenager: I would complain about some inevitability of
my existence that seemed, then, intolerable – getting out
of bed, going to school, being polite to distant uncles
who hadn't seen me since I was yay high – and she would
give me a look that was part pity, part amusement, part
murderous frustration. It would propel me, somehow,
through whatever it was that I did not want to do.

'I'm sorry,' Joyce says, 'but you have to upgrade if you
want to stay enrolled on the programme.'

By now, Joyce and I have reached a sort of truce: I

won't openly complain about the things she asks me to do, and she will not push me to do anything more than is absolutely necessary. The other members of my cohort, the ones who want to be real academics one day, seem to exist in a constant rotation of seminars and conferences and writing papers for journals. This, though, is not my life. I go to the library, and then I go to the gym, and then I come home. Joyce has come to, if not accept, then at least tolerate, the fact that I am not like those other, earnest, industrious, ambitious Ph.D. students. She knows that I am a writer, but not, by nature, an academic writer, and that the only academic events or gatherings that interest me are American ones that take me closer to Max.

'It's fine,' I say. 'I'll get the work together.'

You should expect to submit a substantial body of work of 15–20,000 words, ideally including two or more substantive draft chapters, and a methodological or research framework. You will then have a thirty-to-sixty-minute interview with your Ph.D. committee, on the basis of the materials submitted. The committee's comments at a relatively early stage of the dissertation writing reduce the chance of major problems arising in the student's work later on.

I sift through the various pieces of writing I have put together in a word document called, optimistically, 'thesis.docx'.

Recently I have been working on a chapter about Spiritualism. One of the things the nineteenth-century artists and writers did when they were together in Rome was hold séances. They would sit down in darkened rooms, in the presence of self-proclaimed 'mediums', and try to contact the dead. William Wetmore Story thought he might himself have the power to channel spirits through his pen in a practice he called 'spirit writing'. Elizabeth Barrett Browning attested to seeing apparitions – disembodied hands, a wreath of flowers that floated through the air and landed on her head – in séances. Harriet Hosmer encountered ghosts in Rome: she wrote to friends about having a conversation with her maid one morning, and learning later that the servant had died in the night; she described a little sprite who ran laughing through her bedroom and out into the sunlight. John Ruskin attended séances in which he demanded to speak to the spirits of dead painters: 'I want to speak to the spirit of Veronese!' he instructed his medium. 'Won't I cross-examine him!' I found all of this quite moving in the source material – the efforts they made to reach the unreachable, their yearning to be friends with long-gone predecessors – but by the time I have passed it through the filter of my own academic prose it seems devoid of interest. Still, I include it, together with some introductory paragraphs about Rome and the conditions it provided the expatriate artists who lived there, in my Upgrade submission.

—

The exam takes place in Joyce's office, the little boxy, white-walled room in which I have learned the art of the awkward silence over the past year-and-a-bit. Now, though, it is not Joyce sitting across the table from me, but two other nineteenth-century specialists from the department. One is the man who led the doctoral seminar, who first pointed out to me that Gaskell had written 'Rome' and not 'home'. The other is a more junior member of the faculty, who seems perpetually nervous, her hands always searching for something to smooth out: her hair, her clothes, the air in front of her.

The upgrade doesn't really matter, I know. I've heard plenty of stories of students who didn't pass on their first attempt. When I ask Joyce about this, she says, 'Sometimes failing a student on their upgrade is a good way to give them a gentle kick up the backside.' I think about my peers at the conferences and seminars and networking events, and then of my own half-hearted days spent procrastinating in the library. It is all right if I don't pass, I tell myself. I don't really deserve to pass. I probably do need a kick up the backside, gentle or otherwise.

Now, in the exam, Joyce is sitting silently in the corner, taking notes. She is allowed to be present, but not to intervene. She fiddles with her pen and glances out of the window, waiting for the examiners' questioning to start.

There will be three possible outcomes to an Upgrade Examination:

1. *Unconditional Pass: you will be transferred to Ph.D. with immediate effect.*

2. *Refer for Further Review: this could be either minor amendments over a defined period of time, or a full repeat of the online upgrade procedure.*

3. *Failure to Upgrade: the upgrade panel will review your registration status on the programme. The review determines whether you should remain at M.Phil., or whether you should withdraw from the programme.*

The male academic is very quiet. He lets the younger woman do all the talking. She has blustered through a series of objections to the formatting of my footnotes and bibliography, and I am leaning, once again, on the formulaic response I developed for the doctoral seminar: 'That's interesting. Yes. I'll take a look at that. Thank you.' I am keen to draw out the formatting discussion for as long as possible: the more time we spend on the foot-notes, the less we have for them to tear apart the content of my chapter. But the woman's attention is turning. She is leafing back through her printout of my submission.

'I've read all your work,' she says, 'and I have to say, I'm still not entirely sure I understand what your point is.'

'My point?'

'Your argument. What is it, exactly, that you are trying to say?'

'I want to say . . . I'm trying to say . . . I'm writing about ways of being close to people,' I say. 'I'm writing about the places where artists come together, and the ways they obtain closeness.'

'And they "obtain closeness" in Rome?'

'Yes. Artists and writers travelled to Rome to be close to each other, and then, when they were there, they used Spiritualism to try to reach even more of them. Even the ones who had died.'

'In Rome, specifically?'

'Yes.'

'But why Rome? What was special about Rome?'

I look at the male academic. He is gazing sleepily at his notes. This is my chance, I think, to wake him up, to bring him back into the room. If he is not interested in my work, then he should at least be interested in his own impact on it. Rome is the connecting thread that runs between us, the reason I abandoned my 'unreachable Americas' project in my first year; it was all on his suggestion.

'I dream I am in America, but it always looks like Rome,' I say.

He looks up. I think he might be about to smile.

'Ah, yes,' the woman says, turning over some pages. 'I saw that quote. But I looked it up, and I'm afraid to say, in the Whitehill edition of the *Letters of Mrs. Gaskell and Charles Eliot Norton* it is given as "I dream I am in America, but it always looks like *home*." '

I am about to correct her, to say, 'No, actually, I think you'll find—' when she slides a photocopy of a page across the table to me and I see it with my own eyes. Home. Not Rome. *I dream I am in America, but it always looks like home.*

I look up at the male academic then, expecting at least a flicker of concern, guilt, conflict, but instead he is staring at me expectantly.

'Yes,' he says. 'So, why Rome? What was happening in Rome that was not happening in, say, Florence, or Paris, or London, or Boston?'

'Why Rome?' I falter.

I can see, in the corner of the room, Joyce fidgeting, twisting her hands in her lap. I'm scared that if I look at her for too long she'll catch my eye. I look down, at the blank expanse of white table between the examiners and me.

'I had to write about something,' I say. 'I had to pick a subject. I picked Rome.'

1857

The Manchester Art Treasures Exhibition

It was the summer of the Manchester Art Treasures Exhibition, and your house was full of guests for weeks on end. When the event had first been announced the previous year, you had invited almost everyone you knew, in a fit of boredom-fuelled enthusiasm. And now everyone who had accepted was, disastrously, true to their word. They arrived. You hosted. You threw dinner after dinner, breakfast after breakfast, and spent hours on end travelling between the exhibition site near the Botanical Gardens in Old Trafford and the house on Plymouth Grove. You became an expert in the key sights of the attractions, a tour guide, like one of those unkempt Italian men who had loitered around the churches and galleries of Rome, offering knowledge in return for a few *baiocchi*; or like Mr Norton, who had always known the most important things, and had made it all interesting. You tried your best, for the sake of your guests, to make it interesting.

It was always busy at the exhibition, even early in the mornings. The huge glass-and-iron building echoed with the voices of visitors, and if you stayed too long you always left with a headache.

You took your more genteel, delicate guests all the way to the back, to the Water Colour Gallery, which had the advantage of being the most lightly visited area of the whole exhibition, and was conveniently located next door to the First Class Refreshment Rooms. Your younger visitors from London preferred the Ancient and Modern Picture Saloons, and you sent them off with Meta to see the Giottos and Botticellis and Raphaels, the Rembrandts and Van Dycks, the Hogarths and Reynolds. Then, you loitered in the central vestibule, amongst the Modern Sculpture exhibits, where you found works you had seen for the first time in Rome.

Mr Gibson's *Hunter and his Dog* was there, and his *Narcissus*, the youth leaning idly to stare at a reflection you could not see. There was work by Mr Hiram Powers, an American who had come to dinner at the Casa Cabrale and thrilled both you and Mr Norton by telling a story about a statue he had dreamed of as a child and then encountered with his own eyes at an archaeological dig in the Campagna. His *Fisher Boy* stood just by the main entryway, trailing empty nets behind him, holding up a shell to his ear. The mood around the statue was so still, the shell so solid and silent, that if you stayed near it the din of the rest of the hall seemed to fade. When your daughters came looking for you, they knew to find you there.

—

You were grateful for the guests, though they exhausted you. Their constant presence meant that you and Mr Gaskell were almost never left alone together, that the coolness that had settled between you was not given a chance to crystallize into frost. When you had come home from Rome to discover the solicitor's notice in the paper, to see your name mentioned alongside words like 'regret' and 'rushed' and 'slander', you had experienced a pure, vibrant kind of anger. It had almost been joyful in its fizzing, icy power. 'I am writing as if I were in famous spirits,' you seethed, 'and I think I *am* so *angry* that I am almost merry in my bitterness, if you know that state of feeling.'

You had fumed and raged at Mr Gaskell for the way he had handled the Lady Scott affair. And he, in turn, had been deathly quiet, had turned away from you and retreated into his study. He condemned you without saying a word, for writing such a rash, haphazard book and then vanishing off to Italy, swanning around the continent with your American friends, leaving him to deal with the consequences. 'I have cried so much since I came home,' you wrote. 'I never needed kind words so much, and no one gives me them.' You had tried, in weaker, sadder moments, to go to your husband, to provoke in him any kind of tenderness, but he had told you only that he had work to do, and that you had guests to entertain.

'I *did so try* to *tell the truth*, & I believe *now* I hit as near the truth as anyone *could* do. And I weighed every line with all my whole power & heart.'

144

Your whole power and heart were ebbing and sad and furious by turn. You wrote to your publisher, suggesting a new foreword: 'If anybody is displeased with any statement or words in the following pages I beg leave to withdraw it, and to express my deep regret for having offered so expensive an article as truth to the public. It is very clever is it not?'

You remembered, one morning, a few seconds after waking up, that you had discussed the Manchester Exhibition with Charlotte the year before. You had given her the dates, and told her that she and her husband would be welcome at Plymouth Grove. She had agreed, and talked excitedly about it more than once. She had been delighted by the prospect. She had wanted to see the Raphaels in particular. She had been curious about the modern painters, too, as her brother had, at one point, aspired to be an artist.

And since then, unthinkingly, you had filled up all your guest rooms and even if she had been alive to visit, there would have been nowhere to put her. The thought caused a pang of guilt that made you turn over in bed and press your face into the pillow, to will yourself to go back to sleep for as long as you were allowed.

It was unusual for you to wake and so rapidly fall into tragic thoughts. For months after your return, you opened your eyes thinking you were in the Casa Cabrale. It was second nature to you to slide out of bed and move to a window that, you were certain, looked out at the stone steps of the tilting street below and the sun angling down onto the Collegio Sant'Isidoro. Soon the chill in the air would encroach on the fantasy, and the dark, grey sky glowering through the glass would puncture it entirely. You sank back under the covers, pulled them right up to your face, closed your eyes, and thought of Mr Norton.

To the lawsuits threatened by Lady Scott were added a new set, mentioned menacingly in pamphlets written by the son-in-law of the master of the school in whose care two of the Brontë children had died. In the face of these aggressions you offered to retract certain of your stronger criticisms of the school, but no sooner was this agreed than Mr Nicholls, Charlotte's widower, became enraged and forbade you to do so. He began writing impassioned articles in the *Leeds Mercury*, accusing the school of far worse than you had dared in the *Life*. The affair seemed interminable, and in spare moments between mealtimes, when your guests were resting, you sat at your desk and began to delete the true things from your manuscript that you were not allowed to say.

You crossed through so many written truths that summer that you began to forget the same was not possible in life. You could not draw a line through your feelings. You could not draw a line through your memories, however much they plagued you, and distracted you, and gave you false hope.

———

Did you wish, sometimes, that you could draw a line through Mr Norton? Not as often as you wished for him to come to you.

You clung to your memories of him, the way the old Catholic ladies in Rome clung to rosary beads. If you loitered long enough around those white Roman statues at the exhibition, you half expected him to emerge from behind one, proffering some useful bit of knowledge, or a suggestion about where to have lunch. At the end of each day, in the carriage on the way home, if Meta or Marianne were with you and carrying the conversation with your guests, you allowed yourself to daydream. You imagined that you were in Italy again, that you and Mr Norton were driving out together across the Campagna, that, just as in your ghost story of the bride who dreamed of the face, your own narrative ended with Mr Norton claiming you as his own and vanishing away with you.

And then the carriage would hit a divot in the road and your head would thud against the board, or Marianne would have a question about dinner, or a neighbour would pass in the other direction and you would be forced to stop and talk. You would breathe in smoke from a nearby factory. You would return to the world.

I have cried so much since I came home. I never needed kind words so much, and no one gives me them. When you wrote to Mr Norton and told him what had happened, how you were, he replied and said, so simply, as though it were the easiest thing in the world, that you should come to

America with him when he left at the end of July. You totted up the reasons you could not go: Mr Gaskell, when asked, refused to consider it; the girls needed supervision; the lawyer's bills after the *Life* were vast and prohibitive.

'I must stay here with as calm a face, and as brave a heart as I can, at any rate for the present,' you wrote back. 'But you can come to us.'

He could come to you, and he should, and he promised he would.

2015

560 Million Years After the Big Bang

It has been six months since I last saw Max in the flesh, and his imminent arrival in London forces me to consider my own body afresh, to scrutinize myself. I look in the mirror and try to view my reflection as he would see me. How am I different from the person I was when we were last together? I feel self-conscious about what has changed – hair is longer and in need of cutting – and what has not changed – the same three bras I wear on rotation – in equal measure.

I pay money I do not really have to people who promise to beautify me. On the day before Max is due to arrive, I flit from the hairdresser to the nail salon to the waxing parlour like a wealthy, bored housewife, and then I buy new underwear. I want to be fresh and exciting to Max. I want to be worth the wait, and worth the journey. I am readying myself.

This is, I know, a distraction. If I focus on my appearance, on my body hair and toenails, I don't have to think about the state of mind of the man for whose arrival I am preparing. I don't have to worry about the fact that his thoughts are tending, more and more, to the difficulties in our relationship; to the fact that his job hunting has so far been fruitless and he is so worried about money that he has moved back in with his parents rather than staying, permanently, with me; to the fact that when he said, that first summer in Boston, that he was *not looking for a relationship right now*, maybe, just possibly, that was his more honest answer; to the fact that the wedding that we had proposed take place in under eighteen months seems implausible, fantastical, a dream.

Without my exactly noticing how, he has changed from the person who made everything OK, to the person for whom I need to make things OK. In the afternoon, I hurtle from my beautification mission to the supermarket to buy the sorts of foods Max likes that I don't normally have: ketchup, beer, almond milk. I want to make everything easy. I want to show him that it will be all right.

As I am walking home with the handles of shopping bags digging into my forearms, he sends a text. I have been waiting to hear from him, anxious for reassurance, and I rush to check the message. It is a link to a BBC news story about the Big Bang. *Look at this.* I stop in the middle of the pavement and stare at my phone.

Stars did not appear in the sky, the article says, until 560 million years after the Big Bang. For 560 million years, the universe was dark and blank; then, slowly, stars began to form. The first stars are 100 million years younger than previously thought.

The article comes with a video, like an old-fashioned screensaver, in which shooting stars dart towards the screen. It makes me feel seasick. I do not know what, exactly, Max is trying to say.

That evening, in a spotless home with fully stocked fridge, I call him. Now is the time, I've decided, to be positive; to put to one side the angst-ridden conversations of the past few weeks, the long anthologies of Poems of the Day that I've been waking up to find in my inbox. Tonight, the thing to do is to remind Max, and to remind myself, that we will be happy again once he gets to London.

He answers the Skype call. I smile.

'Hi,' I say.

'I need to tell you something,' he says, and my stomach turns.

M: *I have been thinking a lot about the state of my life and the impact it is having on the people I love – on you.*

      N: *Don't you dare do something awful and tell me it's for my own good.*

M: *It would be though.*

      N: *We can talk about all of this when you get here. Just get on the plane.*

M: *I'm sorry. I can't.*

      N: *Can't what?*

M: *Can't get on the plane.*

N: *You're not coming?*

M: *I'm sorry.*

N: *You're not coming?*

In the morning, Holly lets herself in and finds me curled up underneath the coffee table in the living room. I am not sure when I put myself there. I haven't slept, haven't been able to get myself to bed, or think about Max, or think about anything that isn't Max, and at some point overnight I must have crawled onto the floor. Holly takes my hand and tries to help me up, but my hips get wedged under the table and I can't move.

'How did you get under there?' she asks, and I can see from her expression that she doesn't know whether it is all right to laugh, and then moments later understands that it is not.

She makes me coffee that I do not drink. She sits next to me on the sofa and says nothing, and then, occasionally, small, comforting, forgettable things. *I'm so sorry. He's an idiot. I'm so sorry.* I stare at my immaculate fingernails, and splay out my pedicured toes, and run my fingers through my hair, which is smooth all the way through; no split ends after yesterday's cut. If I hadn't been awake all night, if I wasn't dehydrated and puffy-faced from bawling, if I wasn't deconstructed by grief, I'd be looking lovely today.

Louise and Izra arrive, with chocolate, wine, soup. Other friends stop by to check in and contribute to the mountain of comfort food that is growing on my kitchen counter.

It feels as though my ears are ringing, as though my hearing has been blocked: I am not in the room with the people who have come to look after me. I know they are all here, but they seem distant, faint, as though I am behind glass. Holly, Louise and Izra take shifts babysitting me, cooking, persuading me to eat, reading in silence in the corner of the room and occasionally looking over at me, saying nothing, or saying, 'OK?'

They listen to me repeating the same things over and over again: 'How could he do this? Why is he doing this? How could he?'

Later that week, when the news has reached my family, my father sends me a little blue cake, with a pattern of raindrops and umbrellas iced onto it. It is the most melancholy cake I have ever seen. My brother and his girlfriend, Alice, send a fancy tin of hot chocolate. My mother comes to London and buys me lunch, and then dessert, and then coffee, and throughout the whole meal I just cry, alarming the diners at next-door tables and the waitress, who doesn't know where to look when she brings over plates.

My chest hurts. My whole body hurts. My heart is broken.

My heart is broken.

1858

Séance

Harriet was hosting, but she felt as nervous as a guest at an unfamiliar house. She had spent all day preparing, readying the apartment, the drawing room, the little four-legged table and the chairs positioned around it just so. She had read as many books as she could find on the subject, to ensure the conditions were right: no light must enter the chamber from outside; there must be absolute silence in the rest of the house. The hearts of the participants should be open and calm. They should not bring with them anticipation, or scepticism, or disdain. The spirits sensed these things, and kept away. The petty longings and jealousies of the living had a repellent effect upon the dead.

In her own household, recently, there had been too many petty longings and jealousies to count: the happy sanctuary for female bachelors that had comprised herself, Emma, Matthew and Charlotte was not quite happy any more. Charlotte was heartbroken: Matthew, her companion of ten years, had abandoned her after a violent row and returned to America. Worse, still, the cause of the row had been jealousy over Charlotte's relationship with Emma, which Matthew had suspected – not wrongly, Harriet thought – of being too close. Now she, Harriet, who had once been involved with Matthew, was sharing her bed with Emma. She and Emma were wives, Harriet liked to think, though she was as troubled as Matthew had been about the way Emma and Charlotte looked at each other.

In short, Harriet thought, as she moved around their apartment, touching the table top, the lamps, the heavy curtains, the spirits had obstacles to overcome. She tried to imagine how the room would seem through the medium's eyes: porous, a threshold, not the stone-and-mortar backdrop to volatile domestic drama that it seemed to her. For now, it was still just a room, still the place where she and Emma and Charlotte squabbled and disagreed and loved each other and sat in the evenings to read, but soon it would be a vessel for ghosts.

She tried as best as she could not to hope too much, and yet she spent the day in a state of emotional preparation. She caught herself that afternoon looking at her own reflection in the mirror in her studio, pulling awkward faces and playing around with her hair. She told herself that the evening would be a success if only the living guests came, and the medium performed; if there was even the slightest evidence of the supernatural at work in her drawing room. And yet her heart was giddy, excited: she was hoping against hope for a reunion.

The Storys were the first to arrive, Mr Story uncharacteristically serious, Mrs Story sweet and distracted as ever, glancing around as though she was visiting for the first time, commenting on the lovely furnishings, the beautiful artwork on the walls, although she had breakfasted there just last week.

'You look beautiful, Harriet, dear,' she said, and reached out a hand to stroke one of Harriet's curls.

Harriet, normally annoyed when Mrs Story flirted, felt warm to her then, grateful for the reassurance.

'Is he here?' asked Mr Story.

He could have meant Mr Powers, or Mr Hawthorne, who was also expected, or the medium, Mr Home, but before Harriet could clarify which, Emma arrived, still dusty from a day's work in her studio, and Mr Story began at once to ask her about the bust of Charlotte she had been working on all spring. By the time Charlotte herself came down from her bedroom, stretching after a nap and full of cat-like yawns, Mr Powers had arrived, and so had Mr Hawthorne and, unexpectedly, Mrs Hawthorne, too. The room felt overcrowded, and Harriet hovered at the edge, watching, listening.

There was an oddly severe air to the gathering, even once they were seated in the parlour and taking refreshments, even after Charlotte had valiantly filled the silence with a recitation from *Richard II*. It was a consequence, perhaps, of the mix of personalities and moods present: Charlotte was sad though pretending not to be, Emma was tired and unsmiling, and Mr Story, who always smiled, seemed not to be smiling tonight. Mrs Story and Mr Powers were talking in low voices, glancing at the door, and the Hawthornes both seemed shy, murmuring only to each other.

People were wary, Harriet knew, of the medium she had invited: he had earned himself a reputation as either the greatest spiritualist of the age, or the greatest charlatan on the Continent, depending on who you asked. Mr Browning insisted on the latter, while Mrs Browning professed herself utterly charmed and convinced by him. Harriet had not mentioned to either of them that she had invited him to her house.

'He's late,' said Mr Story.

Harriet had met Mr Home in Florence, where he had held a séance for Hiram Powers. He was a slight, sickly looking American with a childlike manner and high-pitched voice. She had noticed the way he sat timidly on the edge of his seat, how his hand, when she reached out to shake it, was limp in hers and prickly with rings. He seemed afraid of taking up space, afraid to fill out the edges of his own body. If she were to make a statue of him, she thought, it would only be in clay, never marble: he was too diffident to be made permanent in stone.

Perhaps it was this living ghostliness of his that drew the spirits to him. Over the course of that evening in Florence, he had successfully channelled the spirit of his own mother, of Mr Powers' childhood maid, and, most triumphantly, of Samuel Taylor Coleridge.

He had told her that he was coming to Rome to learn the art of sculpture, and she had suggested that while he was there he might teach her a little about communicating with the dead. Who, after all, did not miss somebody?

Who, if given the slightest chance, the smallest hope, would not attempt to reach the people who were gone?

When he finally arrived, Home refused food and drink, and instead hovered palely at the edge of the group, saying almost nothing and stifling the already subdued attempts at conversation, until Harriet suggested they go through to the drawing room. Home went first, and she watched him moving around the corners, inspecting the window frames, prodding the table to check it didn't rock. He was like a curious dog, she thought, sniffing new surroundings, unable to settle.

'The curtains are thick,' she said. 'They don't let through any light. And I had the maid bring this to lay along the floor beneath the door.' She gestured at a bolster, taken from one of the guest rooms, ready by the threshold.

'This is acceptable,' said Home, after a long silence. 'This is sufficient. We will speak to the spirits tonight.' He eased himself lightly down onto the chair at the head of the table. 'Please,' he said, gesturing at the other seats, and Harriet sat meekly, feeling suddenly that she was no longer in her own house, but in Home's.

Emma was beside her, reaching for her hand, and they held each other tightly as the other guests took their places.

'Have your maid take out the lamps,' said Home, softly, and Harriet repeated the instruction at a regular volume to the girl. In the darkness, Harriet focused on

Emma's hand in hers, the throbbing pulse transmitted from the base of the thumb.

They placed their palms flat on the table and waited. Mr Home let his eyes close and his head drop to his chest. Harriet listened for the ticking of the clock, then remembered she had taken it out of the room that morning. She couldn't tell how much time was passing, was only aware of her breath sliding in and out of her nostrils, and of the grain of the wood beneath her fingertips. Once, Mr Story shifted in his chair and exhaled loudly, and Harriet jumped. And then – after how long? Fifteen minutes? Half an hour? – the table leaped.

Charlotte shrieked and there was a moment of confusion while everyone readjusted their seats, and then Home's reedy voice drifted over them all, as though he was not at the table but somewhere above them: 'If any of our spirit friends are here will they signify it by tilting the table again?'

Harriet waited, and then the wood beneath her hands jerked.

'Will the spirits give a communication tonight?' Another tilt. 'To which of us will the spirits give a communication? Let us go around the table and ask.'

She listened to her friends' uneasy voices as they said, one after the other, 'Is it with me that the spirits wish to speak?' and then she said it herself, and was filled with a certainty that it was indeed her, that her little dead brothers, her sister, her mother, and another face,

Margaret, a girl from Harriet's childhood, whom she had loved in a way she had loved nobody since, that all of them were clustered together in the room. The space felt pregnant with news and messages and tender advice.

'Is it with me that the spirits wish to speak?' she asked, and the table jolted so violently that she was almost knocked from her seat.

'Will the spirits indicate by the alphabet the message they wish to relay to Miss Hosmer?' said Home.

A twitch.

Home said, 'A,' and paused. Nothing. Then, almost before he had shaped the letter 'B' in his fluttering, sing-song voice, the table moved.

'So, B,' Emma said.

Home began again from the beginning, reaching, this time, 'E' before the table tilted.

'Be,' said Emma.

In this way the message progressed, painfully, gasp-ingly slowly, while Harriet's heart thudded so sturdily in her chest she thought the sound filled the whole room, until the letters L, O, V, E and D were selected, and Emma said, warmly, 'Be Loved,' and Charlotte said, 'No, no, *beloved*,' and looked triumphant.

For a moment, Harriet took her hands from the table and looked up at the dark ceiling.

'Margaret? My love?' she said. 'Are you there?'

That night, once Home and the guests were gone, and she was lying in bed next to Emma, Harriet was still smiling.

'I really felt her there,' she said. 'I felt her in the room.'

Emma reached out a hand to touch Harriet's face, moving hair back behind her ear. They were silent while they looked at each other. In the candlelight, Emma's face seemed older; she looked tense. Harriet could hear Charlotte moving around in her room next door, the floorboards shifting against each other. Then Emma rolled onto her back.

'I saw him tilt the table,' Emma said. 'Home. I saw him with my own eyes. He did it with his knee.'

'No,' said Harriet, 'you're mistaken.'

'I'm not mistaken, Harriet.'

'It was dark in the room,' Harriet said. 'How could you possibly be sure of what you saw?'

'There was light enough to see him fool you.'

'I know that Margaret was there,' Harriet said.

She turned to face the wall, breathing heavily. She couldn't look at Emma, at Emma's eyes catching the candle's flickering, and at the world as Emma's eyes saw it. How bleak to think that nothing had happened that night but charlatanry and artifice, to think that the people who had left were truly gone, to hear no answer when you called.

2015

Pig–Human Relations in
Jude the Obscure

The rest of the world has not stopped. My friends continue to go to work, and come home again, and make plans for drinks on Friday nights. I can still hear my neighbours having sex on the other side of my bedroom wall. The King's library sends me weekly reminders to return overdue books. It all seems strange, and cold, and unfamiliar. When I was with Max, I loved the certainty of love, and now that that is gone, the other, ongoing regularities of life seem jarring.

And yet I am still expected to participate in the world. I drag myself to meet Joyce, who takes one look at my swollen eyes and blotchy face and says, 'What's happened? Is it the American?'

There are other obligations. Second and third years in the English department no longer attend the doctoral seminar; instead, we are divided into groups by period of specialization, and attend 'Work in Progress' seminars. The Medievalists are put with the other Medievalists, the Early Modernists with other Early Modernists. The doorsteps-in-Dickens girl and I are siphoned off into the Victorianist group. We gather once a month to read and review each other's chapters and conference papers. The work is circulated in advance, and for each meeting, a student is nominated to provide a formal response. Two weeks after Max does not get on the plane, I am due to respond to a paper entitled 'Pig–Human Relations in *Jude the Obscure*'.

This paper addresses the urgent and intricate power dynamics at play in portrayals of pig–human interactions in Victorian literature. I will focus in this instance on depictions of the two species in Thomas Hardy's Jude the Obscure *(1895). Analysis of pig–human relations in this novel reveals a complex dynamic of mastery and sympathy that echoes and illuminates the writer–reader relationship.*

I have glanced at the document, but haven't fully taken on board its subject matter, nor engaged with the idea that I need to formulate a coherent response to it. Instead, I have been focusing on a plan to persuade Max to let me come to Boston. I have spent my Skype-free, empty evenings alternately howling on the kitchen floor and crafting an email.

> I would like to come to Boston. Just for a few days.
> I would sort out my own place to stay, and I wouldn't
> expect you to spend all your time with me while
> I'm there. I wouldn't come demanding anything, or
> expecting any specific answers from you. I don't want
> to disrupt your life or upset you. I just want to see you.

I need to talk to you, in person, in the same room. I need to have a real conversation with you. What do you think? Would you meet me? Please tell me honestly. I hope you are OK.

The subtext here, which Max will understand, is: I don't believe you have it in you to break up with me to my face. I think the reason you didn't get on the plane is that you wouldn't be able to do it in person. And if you can't do it person, then maybe you shouldn't do it at all.

After I press send, I jump every time my phone buzzes. When I check to find that the notification is in fact a message from a retailer announcing a sale, or from the bank telling me my online statement is ready to view, or from anybody who isn't Max saying anything that isn't 'yes, get on a plane to Boston', I am crushed. I refresh and refresh my inbox. Then, seventy-nine hours after I write to him, as I am trying and failing to focus on reading 'Pig–Human Relations in *Jude the Obscure*' for the seminar the next day, the reply comes.

Thank you for writing. I'm OK. It won't stop snowing, but I'm OK. Sorry it has taken me so long to respond. I wanted to think through everything before I wrote back. I've been agonizing over it, and I still don't have the perfect response, but I didn't want to wait any longer before writing. Of course I want to talk to you and do whatever I can to make this easier. But I'm not sure that visiting would be a good idea. First, it would be very expensive. I'd feel guilty about you putting all that money on a credit card just to come to Boston for a couple days. Second, all this feels as if it just happened. I'm still trying to understand it and adjust to it. I worry that I won't be able to say the right things or to make you feel any better.

It has not occurred to me, since I first thought of sending my email, or in the hours I've spent waiting for Max's response, that he would say I should not come. I thought he might be reluctant, I thought he might try to dissuade me, but I did not think he would say no.

I am a new inhabitant of this upside-down world in which Max's role is to do and say the opposite of what I want. So recently, he was the person who could most reliably delight me, the person I turned to when I had desires to be fulfilled.

And now he says I should not come. He does not want to see me.

I argue that farmyard animals, and pigs in particular, are overlooked in contemporary critical discussion of nineteenth-century fiction. The dismissal of pigs as a meaningful focus of critical attention risks limiting and distorting our understanding of how power, violence, care and husbandry operate in Victorian literature.

I am in a state of disoriented desolation when I arrive at King's to attend the Work in Progress seminar on

'Pig–Human Relations in *Jude the Obscure*'. The meeting takes place mid-afternoon, and there are some room-temperature bottles of white wine set out on the table, next to a box of grapes and a plate of homemade flapjacks that one of the third years has brought in. By the time I get there, most people have already assembled and are sitting around being extremely polite to each other.

If there is one defining feature of all the Victorianist Ph.D. students at King's, it is that they are aggressively nice. They are so nice, in fact, that when they see me, red-eyed and tragic-looking, they ask me if I am all right, and the question makes me want to burst into tears. I squeeze my lips together to stop them trembling, and manage to mumble something about being tired.

The author of 'Pig–Human Relations' is wearing a sweater patterned with winged piglets. People are thrilled by this, and point it out to every new arrival in the room. 'Have you seen Victoria's sweater? Isn't it cute?'

I give Victoria and her sweater a half-hearted smile. I look at my page of notes on her paper. At the top I have written 'Why pigs?' This line of enquiry came to me in a moment of desperation, when I recalled my upgrade exam and the flabbergasting question, 'Why Rome?' Underneath that, I have made some brief notes about Foucault, and in particular the author's accusation that Foucault is not only androcentric, Eurocentric and sexist, but species-ist because he focuses so relentlessly on humans rather than animals. I also point out that there are some mentions of pigs at the beginning of *Jude the Obscure* whose role in the novel the author has neglected to analyse, and that in a paper relying on somewhat scant evidence in the source material, this seems like an oversight.

The innate violence involved in relations between pig farmer and pig in the novel is entirely ignored in the Foucauldian model of 'power of care'; Foucault's inherent speciesism thus complicates our understanding of his formulation of power dynamics between humans. Jude's violent encounter with a pig forces him to reassess his masculinity and by extension his relationship to other people. Jude the Obscure is a novel in which pigs are slaughtered, dismembered, weaponized and consumed by humans, and yet, following encounters with pigs, the human characters find that they, too, have been transformed.

I stumble through my notes on the paper. I am neither compelling nor coherent. It is standard to speak for around a quarter of an hour, but after I have gone through each of the points I've prepared, I look at the clock and see that only five minutes have passed. I glance around at the assembled group, who are watching and wondering, perhaps, whether I have another page of notes I'm about to produce.

'Those are all the formal comments I have,' I say. 'But Victoria's paper has provoked a broader question I'd like to put to the group. To what extent can we hold a writer or a critic accountable for what they do not say?'

Mercifully, they take the bait. The doorsteps-in-Dickens girl leaps into a discussion about silence and the interpretation of silence across time. By the time people have run out of things to contribute on this topic, attention has shifted well away from me. People begin asking Victoria more specific questions about pig–human relations in *Jude the Obscure*, and I am free to sit back, and look out of the window, and think of all of the people in the city outside who are doing real things and going to real places, and about Max, on the other side of the Atlantic, not saying things, thinking things that are no longer accessible to me, that I am not allowed to know. *What are we doing?* I think, when someone points out that Victoria's analysis could be broadened to include human interactions with pig fat and lard. *What are we doing?* Victoria notes that the role of the author and the farmer are aligned in their relationship to a flock, herd or drove (of words, of animals) that is both active and submissive. She points to the phrase 'woolgathering' (indulgence in fancy or dreamy imagining) as evidence of this and notes that she has begun work on a new chapter focusing specifically on sheep. We are a group of grown adults sitting around drinking wine in the middle of the day and talking about fictional pigs as though it was a reasonable, normal thing to do.

I slide my phone out of my bag and check it surreptitiously underneath the table. Two new emails. My heart thuds. Max. Perhaps Max has changed his mind about seeing me in Boston.

I open my inbox. The organizers of a conference on 'Nineteenth-Century Female Relationships', which takes place in New York in June, have found funding to fly me there to join them. Next: the Harry Ransom Center in Austin, Texas, which holds the archives of William Wetmore Story, has offered me a four-month fellowship to conduct my research there.

These are things I applied for when I was looking for ways to get to, and spend time in, America, when Max and I were on the same page about the benefits of being in the same country. Now that I have been firmly uninvited by Max, they arrive, like forgotten boomerangs that have returned to hit me in the face.

2015

Saliva Study

I am sitting on the twenty-fifth floor of the Tower Wing in Guy's Hospital at London Bridge, and a dental assistant is dribbling lactic acid onto my tongue with a dropper, then sucking spit out of my mouth with a tube. The acid fills my mouth with saliva and I have to resist the urge to swallow as I lie back with my mouth open, staring at the pattern of ceiling tiles above me, and the triangles of darkness where they have come loose.

We would like to invite you to take part in a study being conducted for a Ph.D. in Mucosal and Salivary Biology. You should only participate if you want to. Please take time to read the following information carefully. Talk to others about the study if you wish.

The goal of this study is to collect salivary proteins from individuals who have not suffered from dental erosion. These proteins act as a barrier that protects against dental erosion. Saliva and tooth enamel from patients who have experienced dental erosion has already been collected. We are investigating what occurs when this saliva and tooth enamel is exposed to healthy salivary proteins.

—

Once the first round of saliva collection is completed, I am given a mouth guard to wear: it was moulded on my last visit to the Dental Research Unit, and has been fitted with enamel from other people's teeth. I try not to look too closely as the assistant produces it. I close my eyes, open my mouth, and nod when the man says he'll be back to take it out in an hour's time.

When he has gone, I sit, swallowing compulsively, and then I get out my notebook. I should spend the spare time working. I should jot down some thoughts about the way my nineteenth-century artists used spiritualism in Rome as an alternative mode of collaboration, a similar kind of distance-bridging effort to the journeys they had made to reach Rome from their homelands. I am participating in the study in the hope that it will inspire a new, matter-of-fact approach to my own research: the student of Mucosal and Salivary Biology researches teeth and I research books and perhaps I can convince myself that those two things are not so different after all. Instead, my tongue still squirming from the sting of the acid, I begin a letter to Max.

Dear Max,

I have written you so many letters. Most of them start by claiming that I don't know what to say, and then somehow go on for several pages, saying things. I have them saved in scraps and pages on my computer, scribbled in the backs of notebooks. Maybe one day I'll try to make sense of them; probably they will quickly become irrelevant. None of them are the right thing to send now.

The reason I do not know what to say – and then go on to say so much – is that for the past few weeks I have been oscillating between love and rage. These two emotions turn on themselves, over and over again. The more I love you, the more I rage against the person who took you away from me so incomprehensibly, who is also – you. I walk around London in a fog of love for you, and then, inevitably, predictably, as I sit on the bus home, I feel myself sliding into fury. I spend the rest of the day stinging with anger. Today, I woke up feeling simply and warmly in love you with again. I will stay like this for a while, and then the pattern will repeat: the magnitude of the loss will catch up with me and I will be overtaken by hurt and resentment.

When I am loving, I read the things I wrote to you when I was angry and feel ashamed of myself for being so thoughtless, selfish, unsympathetic, self-righteous, entitled. When I am angry, I read the loving letters and think how spineless and cringing and pathetic I was to have written them. And so, what follows is not really a letter. It is just a collection of paragraphs. It is a fraction of the things I wish I could say.

I hold my missing of you in my body. I feel it in my stomach and my neck and my skin. I ache so strongly for your hands and lips and breath and voice that I feel bruised. My every impulse is to get on a plane to see you – and then I remember that you refused me that. You told me not to come. You said that you would not have been able to express any more in person, that it wouldn't be worth the expense of the flight, but it is an insult to your intelligence and mine to suggest that communication would be no easier if we were on the same side of the Atlantic. You cannot deny that of all the things that came between us, the most damaging was the simplest: the miles.

There are so many things I want to tell you: news, ideas, dreams, things that have changed. It is my first impulse to tell you, whenever anything happens. And then, almost at once, I swallow that urge. All the things I want to say, all those reaching hands, are slapped away, almost as soon as they appear. I know if I were to tell you, you'd say, 'That's great,' or 'I'm really happy for you,' like a distant friend, like someone who is not at all involved or affected. You started doing that a few weeks before we broke up and it hurt, although I didn't understand why at the time. I can't bear to hear you do it again.

I saw a baby on the tube yesterday, very new, all scrunched up in its father's arms, fist clenched around his little finger. It hit me that what I have lost is not just you, not just the future I thought I would have with you, but our children, too. I had begun to believe in them. Now they are gone. They were going to exist and now they never will. The baby on the tube and its father got off at Oxford Circus, and I watched them walk right down the platform and take the exit for the Central Line.

Everything beautiful makes me think of you.

I miss sending you poems. I miss waking up to poems from you. I still have the instant thought, whenever I come across something I like, that I'll send it to you. At first, I saved those things in a long, strange anthology on my computer. Then I deleted the file and now I can't remember what was in it. My mind keeps coming back to the last poem I sent you, the night before you broke up with me – Elizabeth Barrett Browning's 'Sonnet 14' – and wondering how you could possibly have read it and still have done what you did. Perhaps you found it banal.

A few days after you told me you didn't want to be with me, the *New York Times* published a story about how to deal with a break-up before Valentine's Day. In the article, various writers described their experiences of heartbreak and their advice for recovery. Some were better than others. It was a perfectly average piece, but at the time it struck me as miraculous.

What I am trying to say is that I want to go home. Because you are home for me. You are the person with whom I most clearly recognize myself. I feel cast adrift, horribly homesick, being cut off from you. And I thought I was – I can't help but believe I still am – that person for you, too. I wish you would come home.

I dreamed that you and I were trying to go on holiday, but everything was going wrong. It was one of those frantic, panic-stricken dreams in which you cannot get where you need to be and everything is upside-down. I turned up at the airport without my passport. I had to go back for it, but you had already gone through security. When I got home, I discovered a child in my bedroom, turning all the lights on. I found my passport, and the only thing I had to do was figure out how to turn off the lights, but there were bulbs everywhere, and switches everywhere, and every time I tried one it would illuminate a different part of the room. There were twenty minutes to go until departure time. I called you. You said it would be all right, I would definitely make it. And I was still on the phone with you as I watched the flight take off. I knew you were on it, without me, but still you kept saying that I was going to get there in time, that everything would be fine, even as the plane disappeared from view.

There was a night last summer when we sat out on the beach on Cape Cod in the dark with a bottle of wine. I was in love with you. You were in love with me. It seemed very simple. I was getting cold, and I told you so, and you said we should go inside. We went back to the cottage. That was it. And now I keep thinking about that moment, how casual I was about cutting it short, how certain I was that we would have countless other opportunities to sit out on the beach in the dark and drink wine together. If I had had the faintest suspicion of what would happen a few months later I would have stayed on that beach with you all night.

Nell

The assistant bustles back into the room, glances at my notebook and says, 'Ooh, looks like you've been making good use of your time.'

The mouth guard makes it impossible to speak or smile, for which I am grateful. I shrug.

'So you're doing your Ph.D.?' he says, as he reaches over to slide the guard out. It comes loose, trailing saliva.

'Yeah,' I say, wiping my mouth and running my tongue over my teeth.

'Never a moment to lose, huh?' the assistant says, looking a second time at my scribblings on the page.

After another round of acid-induced-saliva collection, I leave the hospital with a piece of paper confirming that I will be paid two hundred pounds for my participation in the study, and a bitter taste in my mouth.

1857

The First of Many

There was nothing for it but for them to meet: your husband and Mr Norton. Two halves of your life were set to close around you, in the genteel arena of the house on Plymouth Grove. The visit was the result of a long negotiation: you had suggested dates to Mr Norton but he had written to say he was needed elsewhere; he had suggested dates to you but for days when your guest rooms were already occupied. In the end, he had moved prior engagements around to make time for the visit. You had insisted that he come while the Art Treasures Exhibition was in Manchester, and so, dutifully, he did.

The morning Mr Norton was expected, you couldn't sit still. You paced between the parlour and the kitchen, annoying Hearn. You called the housemaid, Mary, to check the guest room was ready, and when she said it was, you told her to clean it a second time. Marianne looked out from her room and said, 'Oh, mama, please, no more guests! Are you not tired of being agreeable? I do so want leisure to sulk and be silent in.'

'It's for Mr Norton,' you said, and your daughter's expression softened.

'Oh,' she said, 'in that case, I don't mind.'

Even Marianne, it seemed, was not immune to Mr Norton's charms, and the memories of your Italian days he would bring with him.

You tried to see your house the way he would see it. Would he notice the newly upholstered furniture, the tasteful wallpaper, the Indian rugs, all paid for with the proceeds from *Mary Barton* and *Ruth*? Would he want to see the corner of the table where you wrote, ink-splattered and covered in the ongoing edits of the *Life*? There were small grooves in the wood where you had pressed too heavily with the pen. You so wanted him to see it, the table and the evidence left on it by your work. You wanted him to look over the revised manuscript and tell you what he thought of it (and you wanted him to take your side, to rage on your behalf over the violence you were being forced to inflict upon your own text). You wanted him to see that you were still a writer here, in Manchester, the same woman who had told him ghost stories all over Rome. You did not want that to be drowned out by the presence of the house, and of the husband.

In Rome, Mr Story had shown you photographs of American houses, with wooden slats instead of bricks, shuttered windows, and dark forests behind. Everything in the pictures had looked new, wild, foreign. You imagined alligators, bears, a menagerie of predators, lurking in the shadows. To Mr Norton, Plymouth Grove would seem solid and flat and safe. Manchester would seem grimy and dull. Perhaps, you, too would seem that way to him, out of the Roman sunlight.

It was hard to believe he would really come, and yet, before you had time to doubt, to fixate on the unlikeliness of it all, there he was, walking in long strides up towards the house. You rushed downstairs to greet him, calling to the girls and Mr Gaskell as you ran.

You opened the door yourself. 'Oh you came, you really came.'

You had half expected that he would seem different in Manchester to the way he did in Italy. Everything seemed dingier to you, more drab. But here he was, unchanged, his face as bright and open as when you first saw it on the Corso, surrounded by the gaiety of the carnival.

He was beaming. 'Is it only two months since I saw you in Rome? It feels like years.'

You were about to agree, to tell him in a rush about a million thoughts and ideas and feelings you had had since then, but you sensed, without turning, that Mr Gaskell was behind you.

Mr Norton's expression became a little more formal as he said, 'Mr Gaskell,' and held out a hand. Your husband stepped forward and shook it.

'I've heard so much about you,' Mr Norton said, which was not a lie, exactly, you thought, but certainly a very generous version of the truth. 'It's an honour to make your acquaintance, sir.'

And just like that, the day was underway, and Mr

Norton was in your house, speaking to your youngest two girls, whom he hadn't met, and reminiscing about Rome with Meta and Marianne, and being deferent and knowledgeable in conversation with Mr Gaskell, asking him about the Cross Street Chapel, and about provisions in Manchester for the working poor. In the afternoon, you left Mr Gaskell in his study where he was happiest, and set off for the exhibition. Once you arrived, you sent the girls to find refreshments so that, just for a moment, you could stand in the modern sculpture court with Mr Norton, and let the crowds stream around you, and pretend that you were in Rome again, that you had just stepped into the Capitoline Museum and that when you walked outside you would do so into bright sunshine and the sound of the *pifferari*'s raucous pipe music.

'How is everyone?' you asked. 'How are Mr and Mrs Story? And Miss Hosmer? Is Miss Beecher-Stowe still there? Has Mr de Vere made any conversions?'

'They all miss you,' Mr Norton said.

'We miss them.'

'It is really not the same at the Casa Cabrale these days. Mr Story was talking, in fact, of moving – the Prince Barberini has offered them rooms at his palazzo.'

'Oh, no! They can't move!' You were horrified at the thought. 'It must always stay the same, exactly as it was. I couldn't bear it if anything changed.'

Mr Norton smiled, but it was not his usual, full, glowing smile. 'I shall pass on your orders to the Storys.'

———

That night, when everyone had retired, you sat alone at your writing table. Above you, in the room you had made Mary prepare and re-prepare for him, Mr Norton was getting ready for bed. He would sleep on your sheets, under your blankets, his head on one of your pillows. After a summer in which your house had been full of guests, it was only now that it struck you how close they were, how intimate it was, to have another person in your house, breathing your air and touching your things.

In the morning he would breakfast with you all, and be witty and charming and make the younger girls fall in love with him and Mr Gaskell think he was a 'serious, clever fellow', and then he would prepare to leave. He would apologize for not staying longer, and say he wished he could, and you would be sorry, too, but optimistic. You were confident that before long, you would go to America. You would see him in his own country, in one of those wooden houses in the dark, American woods. It would be the first of many visits. 'I will see you soon,' you would say. It had been true last time, when he had been the one to say it. It would be true again now, you were certain.

But that night, sitting alone in the room beneath the bed where he was sleeping, you surely wondered about other outcomes, other versions of the story. He was only a few feet away. You could have padded, silently, upstairs. You could have opened his door.

2015

Winning

'Congratulations on winning a tailor-made honeymoon!' The first line of the email is visible before I open it. It is spam, and instead of deleting the message out of hand, I pause to feel sorry for myself, to think how perfectly the universe conspires to prod fresh bruises, to needle raw nerves.

Offer me penis enlargement. Offer me an inheritance from a Nigerian prince. Do not offer me love, or the trappings of love.

Masochistic, embracing self-pity, I open the message. I am the winner of a luxury, bespoke honeymoon to India, it says, including flights, accommodation, personalized itinerary and three romantic excursions of my choice. I am invited to attend the offices of a travel agency in Marylebone, who will be delighted to work with me to create the honeymoon of my dreams. The email is addressed personally to me, and as I read through, despite myself, I begin to feel a creeping interest. I experience a little bubble of excitement at the thought that perhaps something real and hilarious and sort of wonderful has actually arrived, electronically, in the Rare Books Reading Room on a drizzly Tuesday afternoon. I text Holly: 'I think I've won a honeymoon . . .'

On a second read-through, I notice that the email is written in a slightly unusual font, from a woman called Tanya at a PR company whose name I don't recognize. The thrill subsides: it is a scam, after all. I will respond and Tanya will present a once-in-a-lifetime opportunity, and all she will need to secure the booking is my card details. I feel embarrassed to have believed in it for the few seconds when it seemed possible. I think about a friend who, in our first year of university, received an email promising him a cut of several millions of pounds, tied up in Russian bonds, if he would act as a middle man in a complex series of international transactions: he came to my room with a wild glint in his eyes, stammering, momentarily convinced that this was a possibility, that dazzling things could happen to normal people. That was in earlier days of internet scams, before we knew any better. Now: I write to Holly again. 'Wait, no, maybe I haven't.'

I have no memory of entering a contest to win a honeymoon to India, but still, it is undeniably the sort of thing I would have done. All those library days spent sifting through web pages for opportunity and luxury and distraction might have paid off. In recent months I have had other, underwhelming, successes on this front. I won tickets to the London press screening of an action movie marketed at teenage boys. I won a signed print from an artist I neither recognized nor particularly liked.

I google the honeymoon contest, the name of the magazine that ran it, and the hotel group offering the prize. The link to the top result on my search engine is purple, not blue, indicating a site I have visited before. It could be real, then. Have I absent-mindedly and forgettably entered the contest, and then won?

Later I show the email to Holly, Louise and Izra. They are unconvinced but entertained, and cautiously optimistic.

'Reply,' says Izra, 'but don't hand over any identifying information.'

'Don't give them your passport,' says Louise.

Together we craft a response to Tanya at the PR company. I am thrilled, I tell her. I can't believe it! I am available to meet the travel agent later this week.

The first thing the travel agent says when she sees me is, 'Oh, your fiancé couldn't make it?'

I am distracted by my mission to uncover the scam, scrutinizing the office for signs that it is fake, temporary, not a real travel agency. 'No,' I say, and leave it at that. The space, in the basement of a grand building just off Harley Street, is ordinary-looking. The windows need cleaning. There are posters on the walls of the Taj Mahal and tigers emerging from long grasses. Posters, I think – easy to put up and take down at short notice. Two employees sit at desks, tapping at their computers and answering phones. They don't acknowledge me.

The agent takes me into a separate room, brings coffee and invites me to peruse brochures and itineraries and photographs of hotels. She describes the competing attractions of Agra, Shimla, Jaipur. It depends on the time of year, she says; the heat will be unbearable in Delhi before the monsoon. Shimla would be tolerable. I nod and scowl and wait for her to slip up, to ask me for one of the things my friends have forbidden me to hand over.

'When's the wedding?' she asks.

'Next month,' I say, as coolly as I can. She might think she is scamming me, but I am the true con artist here. *Joke's on you, lady*, I think. *There's no wedding at all.*

I tell everyone I know about the honeymoon, sometimes more than once so they have to say, awkwardly, 'Yes, you already said.' I tell my parents and brother, and the other students at King's, and Joyce, and then I tell them all over again. Gradually, cautiously, a question comes back in response to my announcement. Friends look down at their shoes; my mother clears her throat down the phone. Nobody really wants to raise it, but somehow they manage to: 'What if it's real?' they say. 'Who will you take with you if it's real?'

To the list of questions that rotate through my mind – *How could Max do this? How could the future I believed was mine – the marriage, the house, the babies – evaporate so suddenly and so entirely? What did I do wrong?* is added this new conundrum. *Who will come with me on my fake honeymoon?*

When I speak to people at the (fake?) PR company administering the prize, and at the (fake?) travel agent, I fail to stick to one story and instead create an array of love- and travel-related disasters. My fiancé left me at the altar, devastatingly, I tell one woman. To another I explain that I am marrying an American who is in the process of applying for British citizenship, and so his passport is currently being held by the Home Office. My husband is unwell. My fiancé's mother is sick, so he is nervous about being out of the country. We have had to postpone the wedding.

'That's awful,' they say. 'What a tragedy. Poor you.' This is the most genuine interaction we have: they express sympathy for a disaster that feels, to me, not unlike the real, secret one, and I accept their condolences as rightfully mine.

In a state of supreme cognitive dissonance – I believe the honeymoon is hilarious because it is a scam; I believe it is hilarious because it is real – I send an email to Tanya saying that I would like to take my maid of honour in place of my husband. Would that be possible? I have told so many lies by this point that I'm not sure which sob story I have given her previously. But eventually, a reply comes: it is fine for me to take Holly. This seems to tilt the balance of probability towards the whole thing being a scam, because of course they wouldn't mind me taking my fake maid-of-honour on my fake honeymoon that is never going to happen.

And yet I – and Holly, too – still go through the motions of preparation for the trip. At each stage, just when I think they are about to ask for something shifty, they don't. They offer to arrange our visas for us, and ask us to drop off our passports at the office; I write and say that we would prefer to do this ourselves; they say that is fine. They ask us to confirm when we want to fly, and we send the dates, and they write back and say the flights are booked. Would we like to pay extra to extend our trip for a few more nights? If so, we just need to send over our bank details. No we would not, we say, and they tell us that is not a problem at all. I spend the money I earned from the Saliva Study on clothes to take to India. I buy sunglasses and sandals. In the Rare Books Reading Room, I spend hours looking up pictures of the hotels where we will, apparently, be staying: blue swimming pools and gold gilt decor, balconies with views of the Taj Mahal, drops of condensation seeping down the outsides of champagne glasses, with a mountain range out of focus in the background.

When Holly and I board the plane at Heathrow, we look around – at the other passengers and the flight attendants and the images of India sliding past on the seat-back screen – and become hysterical. We are weeping with laughter. We have believed in the reality of the prize enough to pack and come to the airport, enough for Holly to take time off work and for me to tell Joyce not to expect my usual fortnightly update; enough, even, to go to the Indian Embassy and pay for unflattering visa pictures to be taken by an extortionately priced photo booth in the waiting room. And yet we are astonished to find ourselves sitting in seats that are actually, really, truly booked in our names, and for which we have definitely not paid. We are bound for Delhi's Indira Gandhi International Airport.

At some point on the flight, the combination of over-excitement, extended periods of giggling, and several mini-bottles of red wine send me into a murky doze. When I come round, hours later, I peer past Holly to stare out of the window, over the bulk of the aircraft's wing, at the pale creases of a mountain range beneath us. The woman sitting on my other side notices my gaze and says, excitedly, 'Pakistan! It's Pakistan!'

At the Arrivals Terminal in Delhi, a man is waiting to meet us, holding a sign that says, 'Mrs Stevens'. At the hotel, where we are greeted with wreaths of orange flowers and blessings for our health, the false title follows us everywhere we go: 'This way, Mrs Stevens!'; 'How was your flight, Mrs Stevens?'; 'Would you care for some tea, Mrs Stevens?' We are introduced to our butler, and our driver, and the chefs.

In a moment of quiet, Holly mutters, 'Are we supposed to be pretending to be a couple?' and I shrug. I have told so many stories to people in London about our situation, I'm not sure which, if any, has been relayed to the staff in India.

The following morning, while we are eating break-fast, surrounded by important-looking business-people, casually glamorous, talking loudly on phones, the hotel manager introduces himself. He shakes both our hands vigorously and says, 'Congratulations!' several times. He beams. 'Our lucky winner.'

He asks about our itinerary for the day – spice market,

Jama Masjid, an afternoon by the pool – and offers some suggestions about where we can buy rugs. Then, to me, he gives a slight bow and says, 'Mrs Stevens, I am so sorry Mr Stevens could not come.'

I look away. I am uncertain which, of the many meanings his sentence might have, is the intended one. I can feel Holly's eyes on me, waiting for my response. I bob my head. I say, 'Me too.'

Delhi. Rickshaws weave between buses. Street vendors call out as we pass. Sweat slides down the nape of my neck. The air in the spice market is so thick with dust it makes everyone sneeze, and the whole street is loud with the sound of it: a-choo, a-choo, a-choo. A child follows us down an alley, calling, 'How are you, ma'am? How are you?' At the Jama Masjid, a flock of birds swells and shrinks between the arches. Old men doze in the shade. We leave our shoes at the entrance and walk barefoot across ground so hot it burns the soles of our feet, and we have to keep shifting our weight from side to side. We are red-faced and ungainly, sticky, hopping from foot to foot.

Agra. A view of the Taj Mahal from our roll-top bath. Mint juleps on the balcony.

Jaipur. We ride an elephant up to the red fort.

Udaipur. A 'romantic boat ride' out across Lake Pichola; at dusk, bats fill the sky, swerving over their reflections. We eat candlelit dinners by the water, and sleep in a bed doused with petals.

We are living in a picture-book version of a vast and

diverse country. As the days pass, the joyful ridiculous feeling subsides, and is replaced by a kind of sweat-drenched, philosophical anxiety. I lie in a hammock watching Holly swimming in the private pool that surrounds our suite on three sides. *What are we doing here?* I wonder. *How did this happen?* Life is intolerably random. Nothing is certain. The whirrings of a computer award honeymoons to unmarried strangers. The murky churnings of a human mind nudge love to silence with no warning, no logic. Things just happen, without order or reason. *I am so sorry Mr Stevens could not come.*

At the end of the week, we spend a final night in Delhi, from where we will fly home to the rest of our lives, to a world in which I am not a newlywed. I lie awake, my body filled with dread that feels like adrenalin. Beside me, Holly is sighing in her sleep, and beyond our room are the sounds of the hotel at night: occasional footsteps, the faint ding of the lift doors, the clatter of crockery as a bellboy collects a discarded room-service tray. The thought of resuming my solitary London routine is nauseating. I am the opposite of a newlywed: a newlyleft, a newlyalone. I don't want to go back.

In the morning, the driver who takes us to the airport is curious. 'You won a contest to come to India?' he asks. 'You are the winners of a competition?'

'Yes,' I say. 'A contest in a magazine.'

'You are very, very lucky, Mrs Stevens,' he says.

2015

People Who Fit Your Criteria

It is summer and I am in America. Specifically, I am in New York. Specifically: Harlem. After dithering about whether or not to go to the 'Nineteenth-Century Female Relationships' conference, to which I only applied so I could see Max, I decided to attend, and to stay in the city for a while afterwards. From here, I will go directly to Texas to begin a four-month research fellowship at the archives of the Harry Ransom Center.

London had begun to feel toxic. After returning from India, my gloom darkened into something more acute. I started crying on the tube, provoking responses from strangers that ranged from sympathy to alarm. My social life, previously a source of comfort, began to feel like a series of arduous challenges: evenings I had to grit my teeth to get through before I could return to my default state of lying on the sofa in my pyjamas. My friends' patience, too, was beginning to wear thin. There were only so many times I could expect them to listen to me philosophizing on heartbreak, or my plans to persuade Max to come back, before they felt the need to suggest that, a) my problems were not as severe as I thought they were and b) Max was not going to change his mind. Both of these points enraged me, and made me feel bitter and resentful, though I knew they were made for the kindest possible reasons.

It was time for a change of scene. I found a tenant willing to take over my flat for the summer, and rented a sublet apartment on West 113th Street for the same money. I booked a flight. I got on a plane.

My friends in New York, including my brother and an ex-boyfriend from my early twenties, have not yet had their supplies of empathy exhausted by my post-Max misery. Promising, too, is the fact that they are not quite as uniformly coupled-up as my friends in London; for the summer, at least, I will not be the only single person in the room at every social event I attend. There will be new things to do, new people to see, and, hopefully, new feelings to feel. After giving a paper on 'Elizabeth Gaskell's "Story of the Face" and the invisible relations of influence in nineteenth-century Rome', my time is my own in this sweltering city.

I have told Max I am here, of course, and hope, ardently and obsessively, that he will come to New York. In the evenings, I crawl out of the window of my bedroom onto the fire escape, and stare down at the rats tearing through bin liners in the alley below. I try calling Max, and when he doesn't answer, I cry and cry and cry.

Each day I walk from my apartment to the library at Columbia University. It is humid and sticky, even first thing, and I move slowly, my bag always too heavy on my shoulder, leather straps rubbing sweaty skin. I cross

Frederick Douglass Boulevard and buy coffee from the place on the corner, and then enter Morningside Park. There, masochists use the steps that climb its steep incline for their morning workouts. I stop halfway to rest, catch my breath and mop away sweat, while glistening, topless men pass me multiple times on their way up and down, and up and down again. Stray cats emerge from the undergrowth and watch me, wide-eyed and dusty.

I spend the rest of the day in the silent, air-conditioned library, reading about the Roman catacombs discovered by nineteenth-century archaeologists, and working on a chapter that presents nineteenth-century Rome as the artistic equivalent of a coalmine: a resource to be tapped.

Twice a week, I visit Dr Maier, a therapist in her mid-sixties who listens to me ranting and crying over Max and says things like, 'You talk about him as though he has died. You are talking like a bereaved person.'

'I just feel grief,' I say. 'I am grieving.'

'You are talking like a bereaved person,' Dr Maier says again. 'Your depression has twisted this breakup into a kind of death.'

She prescribes me antidepressants. I swallow them and wait: perhaps, miraculously, these drugs will make everything seem all right again, will close up the edges of the gaping hole that Max left in my life. I look around, expecting things to appear different, expecting the light to change. It all looks the same.

'I turn thirty this year,' I tell Dr Maier. 'And I don't have a husband and I don't have a baby.'

'And is that what you want?' she asks. 'A husband and a baby?'

'I got used to the image of myself as someone who could have those things – the things that other people have, the things that everyone is supposed to want. I felt as though they already belonged to me. And now they have been taken away, which probably makes me want them even more. It's perverse, I know.'

'What is it about those things that you think you want?'

'I don't know if I do want them – at least not necessarily the husband. I do want the baby, I think I really do, and the husband, or at least the partner, would make that more straightforward. I want to have the option. I want the option to have the things that other people want.'

'Are you giving yourself the option?' Dr Maier asks. 'Are you dating?'

I go to the offices of a match-making service, where a twenty-something girl called Anisha asks me a series of questions about the kind of person I would like to meet.

'I just want to meet someone who has their life together,' I say. 'Someone who knows what they are doing. Nobody in a crisis.'

'Right,' says Anisha, typing something into her laptop. 'Anything else?'

I rack my brains. I try to think of any other quality that was lacking in Max, the absence of which should have warned me of the inevitable failure of the relationship.

'Maybe not anyone who is lactose intolerant?' I say. 'Someone who can eat cheese.'

'Right,' says Anisha. 'Both men and women?'

'Yes.'

'Height preference?'

'No.'

'Do you have a physical type?'

'Not really.'

'Can you name a celebrity you think is particularly attractive?'

In that moment, I cannot recall the name of a single celebrity. 'Not really.'

'OK,' Anisha says, at the end of the interview. 'I'm pretty sure we have some people on our books who fit your criteria.'

I go on dates with a marketing executive, a technology consultant and a woman who is fund-raising for a start-up that delivers cupcakes to office workers, and then I take the subway to my friend Laura's apartment in Carroll Gardens, and complain to her that I have lost the ability to be attracted to anyone at all. She feeds me tacos and tells me that six months after the breakup is too soon for me to be dating.

'Maybe you're right,' I say. We are drinking margaritas and I am coaxing my mind away from self-absorption and towards the far more interesting, edifying topics: Laura's life, Laura's writing, Mrs Gaskell, the nuclear deal with

Iran. My phone buzzes in my bag. I dig it out and see Max's name on the screen, glowing.

The message: *I'm coming to New York next week.*

I reply: *Do you want to meet up?*

He writes back: *Yes.*

In the lobby of the Ace Hotel, Max and I stand and stare at each other. I don't know how to act, how to be. Should I hug him? A kiss on the cheek? A handshake? My heart is racing. I feel as though I have forgotten how to stand naturally.

'Hi,' I say.

'Hi.' He opts for a hug. His body against mine feels astonishingly solid: a reminder that Max is a real person, occupying space, and not just an idea over which I obsess, not just a series of lines of text on the screen of my computer. He has lost weight since I last saw him; I can feel his shoulder blades through his T-shirt.

'You look good,' I say.

'You look beautiful.' I know him well enough to understand that he will always say this, that he is polite above all else, that I can read nothing into it.

There is nowhere to sit. Every sofa, chair or ledge is occupied. We are surrounded by Apple logos glowing from the back of laptops, an electric orchard. Behind the little white fruits: the illuminated faces of people at work on their novels. It goes without saying, I think; they are all working on their novels, every last one of them.

We go to the bar, where there are two available stools,

but not next to each other. A woman sitting alone in between them notices us hovering awkwardly nearby and moves across, making a big show of sliding her bags and drink over. 'There you go,' she says, loudly, and I smile at her, and notice that she is red-eyed and a little wobbly as she readjusts in her new place.

'How are you?' asks Max, once we're sitting and have ordered drinks.

I don't know how to answer. I think about climbing the steps up through Morningside Park every morning, and about the forced, awkward conversations I made with my dates, all of whom were hand-picked by the match-making agency, all of whom ate dairy, all of whom were pleasant, none of whom seemed interested or interesting. I think about Dr Maier's office with its window looking out at the traffic along Broadway. *You are talking like a bereaved person*, Dr Maier said, and now the ghost of the man I lost is sitting next to me on a bar stool drinking a beer and waiting for me to answer his question.

'I've missed you,' I say.

'I've missed you too,' says Max, and he reaches out and squeezes my hand.

'You guys are so adorable.'

I swivel on my stool to see who has spoken. It's the woman who gave up her seat for us. She has ordered another drink, over which she is leaning unsteadily. She bends to sip from a straw.

'You are the cutest couple,' she says.

'Oh,' I say, 'thanks.' I turn back to Max.

'How long have you guys been together?' she asks.

I turn again and push my stool back from the bar so that Max can see her. I look at him with my lips pressed together in a way I hope communicates: you take this one.

Max, ever the lawyer, chooses his words carefully. 'We've known each other for three years.'

Our new friend, after however many drinks she has had, does not appreciate the subtle clarification in his answer. 'Three years?' she screeches. She looks at me with horror in her eyes. 'You've been together three years and you haven't gotten him to marry you yet?'

'Nope,' I say. 'I haven't.'

She shakes her head. 'What is it?' she says to Max. 'You think she's not good enough for you? Is that it?'

'No,' he says. 'That is not it.'

'You think you're going to find someone better than her? Because let me tell you, buddy, that ain't gonna happen. Can't you see how much she loves you? Can't you see the way she looks at you? You think you're gonna find someone who loves you more than this one?'

Our conversation has attracted the attention of the bartender, who is looking apologetic, and as though he thinks he should intervene.

'That's not it,' says Max.

'Look at her cheeks!' the woman says. 'You think you're going to find someone with cuter cheeks than this one?'

'OK,' the bartender says. 'That's enough. Leave these people be, OK?'

'We're just talking,' she says. 'I'm just saying, he thinks he's going to find someone with cuter cheeks?'

The last we see of the woman, she is being ushered away by a security guard toward the lifts. She leaves a strained silence in her wake. Max takes a gulp from his drink, and I draw patterns with my finger in the ring of liquid left behind by his glass on the surface of the bar.

'So is that it?' I say, eventually. 'You think you're going to find someone with cuter cheeks?'

Part Three

SLEEP STUDY

2015

Treehouse

Looking down from my new bedroom, I can see chickens scratching in the dirt, pecking at grass. A cat is sprawled out in a dusty flower bed, watching the birds and flicking its tail. Dangling from the lower branches of a tree, wind chimes sway silently; there is barely a breeze. Everything is slow, calm. Flies buzz around the window screen.

This is my second week in Austin. I am living in a treehouse. In my haze of depression after the breakup with Max – those months of public crying in London, of weeping in Dr Maier's office in New York – I could barely think as far ahead as my next meal, let alone to where I might stay in Texas. By the time I got around to sorting it out, everything on the accommodation list provided by the university was taken; I sifted through online listings and realized that a treehouse in the back yard of a wind-chime-maker called Norma was the best I could expect to find. I have running water, a fridge, a microwave and air conditioning, which is all I really need. At night, I listen to the scratching of squirrels' feet as they scurry over the roof above my bed.

It is peaceful here, and life is very easy: I take a shuttle bus from outside Norma's house every day to the archives, where they give their research fellows free coffee and office space, and the food in all the nearby cafes is excellent. After days spent reading the letters and journals of William Wetmore Story, I go home and sip wine at the window of my treehouse, watching animals crawl, flutter and swagger around the yard. I have decided that in these four months, I am going to finish my thesis. I am in the third and final year of my Ph.D., and after two and a half years of academic dabbling interrupted by fairly constant obsession with Max, it is time to get it done.

It is eight months since Boston's snow emergency, since that awful Skype call, since Max did not get on the plane to London. It is shocking to realize that his absence no longer shocks me. If there is a hole in my life where he used to be, its edges are smoothed over, no longer jagged. Max and I are still on speaking terms – I call to tell him what I am doing, he calls to talk about a short story he's working on – but these conversations are, for the most part, calm, comfortable, no longer angry. I have absorbed the wreck of the relationship somehow, and though I still worry about my future, about whether, when and how I will ever have a baby, about who, how and when I will date again, the very presence of these questions in my life no longer feels like a catastrophe. I do not know how this has come about – it has happened almost against my will – but it seems I have run out of grief. Sometimes that strikes me as sad in its own way: he was the source of so much happiness, and then so much pain, and now even that is gone.

———

A far more pressing blot on my contentment is that I have developed a constant need to pee. I am spending a lot of time reading and writing, but, it seems, even more time buttoning and unbuttoning my jeans as I run to the bathroom again and again. It is worst at night. Just when I've settled, teeth brushed, lights off, my bladder starts to sting, and I have to scurry out of bed again. In the reading room at the Ransom Center, where comings and goings are observed by the hyper-vigilant staff whose job it is to monitor the readers at all times, my constant bathroom trips are becoming an embarrassment. No sooner have I sat down in the mornings, it seems, than I have to leave again.

I go to a pharmacy and buy little paper sticks that promise to detect a urinary tract infection. I conduct several tests over several days, each time with normal results, before I accept that I do not have a UTI. So: it must be in my head, I think. Maybe my bladder is clinging on to my breakup sadness; maybe my urge to pee is in fact an urge to get rid of the last vestiges of unhappiness left behind by Max. I sign up to do yoga in a little room above a pet-grooming shop: at the start of the class, the teacher places her hands in a prayer position and invites Jesus to join us in our practice. Maybe yoga, maybe Jesus in downward dog, will calm my agitated bladder.

The Harry Ransom Center is a haven for the obsessed. All around us is Texas: dry sunlight, cowboy boots and a new piece of legislation that allows students to carry concealed weapons on campus; country music drifts out of every bar in town. But here, in the archives, are the papers of D. H. Lawrence, Lytton Strachey, Dylan Thomas, Tom Stoppard, and buzzing around them like flies to a corpse are scholars from all over the world.

On Wednesdays, we gather in a stuffy meeting room for the weekly coffee morning. We stand around with paper cups, balancing plates of dry marble cake in our free hands, and we talk about the people whose papers we have come to see. The coffee mornings feel, most often, like a meeting of deputies: we are all there on behalf of someone else. I am representing William Wetmore Story, and I talk to other people about him, and they reply with an anecdote about their own subject, until it becomes apparent that the conversation is not really between me and the other person, but a strange conversation-by-proxy between Story and whoever it is they are researching: Ian McEwan, J. M. Coetzee, Christine Brooke-Rose.

'Story had a theory about drawing,' I say. 'He believed that the proportions for best drawing the human figure were derived from an ancient cabalistic formula.'

'Well of course,' says an earnest young Dutch man, 'Evelyn Waugh actually studied drawing alongside religion. He studied medieval-style illumination.'

When I first started at King's, I looked at the girl with Dickens' signature tattooed on her arm with a kind of horror. She had been so consumed by her subject that it had branded her as its own; she belonged to Dickens just as much as he to her. But in Texas, it is clear that each and every researcher, myself included, is wandering around bearing the standard of their chosen subject. I wave my

William Wetmore Story flag in between mouthfuls of cake on Wednesday mornings. I read his letters, his notebooks, his journals, and at home in the evenings, I write.

There is a melancholy to the archives, too, but it is a comfortable, wistful sadness that feels wholesome compared to the bitter heartbreak that dominated my previous year. Story's notebooks detail ideas and plans, detritus from a busy, living mind that is now gone. In the middle of an essay on the merits and pitfalls of literary translation is a sketch of his infant son, sitting on the floor beside his desk. Beneath a journal entry describing an experiment in spiritualist mind-reading is a drawing of a woman labelled 'Model for Marguerite'. The face of the girl is shadowy, thoughtful, eyes lowered. There is an unsent, unfinished letter to an unnamed recipient, letting him or her know that a flute was left behind when they dined together at the Palazzo Barberini, and that he would give it to the Brownings to take up to Florence when they left the following week.

These papers are a record of what is no longer here: the flute, the owner of the flute, the woman who posed as 'Marguerite', the mind that saw and recorded them all. The infant sitting chubbily on the floor in the pencil sketch grew up, became a man, became old, died. The world Story inhabited, the Rome of my fantasies, in which the great and good of nineteenth-century Letters rub shoulders and throw parties and create works of genius and leave behind musical instruments, has vanished. The people in whose company I have spent so much of the past three years? They are all dead.

Story believed that he could tell the character of a letter-writer simply by holding the paper, without reading a word. I sit with his writing for days on end and wonder if I'm any closer to him, his life, his friends. The notebooks are impossible to read in parts: the handwriting too messy to decipher, or the pages torn. I am terrified, as I leaf through, that the paper will disintegrate under my fingers. Other scholars are given white cotton gloves to wear while reading old material – they look like mimes as, all around me in the reading room, they lift and turn, meticulous and slow, the ancient papers – but the Story archive is considered either not delicate or not significant enough to warrant protective clothing.

I teach myself, over time, to decipher the variety and tenor of Story's moods through his handwriting: the calm, dreamy tilt of his happier moments, the frantic scrawl of a note dashed off in bitterness. Perhaps, after all, I am reaching a kind of intimacy with my subject. And then I find a poem, so messily written that hours of staring at certain words don't help me decipher them.

> *What avails in the end all our striving my friend*
> *I ask what's the use of it all*
> *In struggle and strife we [battle?] through life*
> *And our climbing all ends with a fall*
> *Thought comes to its flower at times for an hour*
> *In a moment – then withers and dies*
> *And strive all we will with our utmost of skill*
> *The [??] we seek, Life denies.*

For at best, what is fame, but a breath of a name
And success, but an empty vaunt
We all are pursuing, in hoping and doing [??]
?? phantoms that lure but to taunt / lurk but to
    haunt?? / Live but to haunt?
Like the waves of the sea [??] [??] [??] restlessly
We strive scarcely knowing for what
But to shirk from life's Light – to be [??] out of sight
To be dashed on Death's shore and forgot.

Later, I read a letter from Mrs Gaskell to Story and his wife, written in September 1857, a few months after she had left their house to return to Manchester. 'It was in those charming Roman days that my life, at any rate, culminated,' she wrote. 'I shall never be so happy again. I don't think I was ever so happy before. My eyes fill with tears when I think of those days, and it is the same with all of us. They were the tip-top point of our lives. The girls may see happier ones – I never shall.'

Will I see happier days? Has my life, at any rate, culminated? I am recovering from a year spent believing that it had, looking backwards as I trudged up the steps through Morningside Park, replaying moments, thinking *I shall never be so happy* as I swallowed the pills prescribed by Dr Maier. But it seems to me that I have reached a point of anticipation again: I can no longer be as certain as Mrs Gaskell was about the trajectory of my life. I can no longer accept without doubt that my happiness has peaked.

So here I am, waiting. I am optimistic. As I sit in the archives opening box after box of William Story's papers, I am full of hope that the tip-top point of my life did not take place in Shu's apartment when Max said, 'I'm going to try something, OK?', was not a moment on the Cape Cod beach with my toes touching his through the sand, but is ahead of me, unknowable.

1859

Sylvia's Lovers

You lapsed into wistfulness. In the autumn, you left Mr Gaskell in Manchester and took a trip to Whitby. From a rugged little cottage on the coast, you gazed out every morning at the grey sea gnawing the grey rocks. You were looking towards the Continent, towards the Netherlands, Germany, Denmark, but you imagined it was the Atlantic you were watching, that beyond the waves and the horizon was America. In the evenings, when the sun sank into the water behind clouds and lit up the sky in pearlescent streaks, you almost thought you saw it.

Twenty-five miles away, in Redcar, Nathaniel Hawthorne was working on a novel you had heard would be about Rome. It was to feature Mr Story's statue of Cleopatra, which you yourself had seen in his studio. There were to be little sketches of all your friends in the city. The thought of Hawthorne being nearby, of the little bud of Italy that was blossoming from his pen, made you think of the place with refreshed intensity. It was a kind of homesickness – you used the German word, *Heimweh*, to describe it – the way your mind took you back, in dreams and daydreams and fantasies, to Rome. When Mr Norton wrote to you, *I revisit in imagination the places to which we went together, I recall our drives & the beauties of the Campagna, I hear your words, & altogether I am passing a very delightful morning with you in Rome,* you knew exactly what he meant. You were there too, at his side.

When the Hawthorne book was published, Norton wrote to you about it: *I know nothing that has ever been written about Italy so admirably true not only to the reality of the country but also to all that it suggests to the imagination. Hawthorne's remarkable fineness of perception & observation, and the intensity of his imagination have enabled him to put into words & to give form to what every lover of Italy & Rome has felt while there, but which very few have been able to express for themselves.*

One morning, as you read *The Times* over your coffee, you saw an announcement that your old friend Eliza 'Tottie' Fox had got married in Rome. She was a painter, and had moved there the previous year, and you had become lazy about writing to each other since then. And now, all of a sudden, she was married. You held the paper in both hands and read and re-read the article. You were unsure what you were feeling.

Marianne wandered into the room and saw your face. 'Mama, are you all right?'

'Yes,' you said, 'yes, look. Tottie has got married in Rome.'

Marianne came over to look at the article, and read it quickly. 'Oh, that's wonderful,' she said, searching your face as though uncertain that this was the reaction you wanted.

'Yes,' you said. 'Yes, isn't it?' Your daughter's words nudged your own emotions in the direction of delight, and soon your confusion left you altogether. You wrote a long, gushing letter to Tottie.

Fancy meeting your fate at Rome. (I dreamt of you and your husband at Albano, in the gardens of the Villa Medici – think of me if you go there.) Where were you lodging at Rome? What were you married in? Roman scarves and cameos? Oh, and is not Rome above every place you imagined? And do you go to the Pamphile Doria gardens, and gather anemonies, and watch the little green lizards as we did?

You tried to tell her, without saying so directly, that you, too, knew what it was to meet your fate at Rome.

Charles Eliot Norton: *We have places here in our circle for you all. Why are you not here to fill them? How pleasant it would be to bid you Goodnight with the thought of meeting you tomorrow at breakfast. It is one of the hopes that I will never give up, that some day or another you will be here. . . . But will it ever be? Today at least my hope is strong.*

Mrs Gaskell: *I wish you would come to see us; every now and then we hear a rumour that you are coming, but you don't come. I – we all – wish you would.*

CEN: *We are not so very far apart after all. – I will imagine myself sitting in your*

213

well-remembered pleasant parlor talking
with you.

> EG: *If you were here I should have such*
> *numbers of things to talk over with you that*
> *scarcely seem worth putting in a letter; a*
> *letter too, that is to cross the Atlantic and*
> *so ought to be full of great subjects, greatly*
> *treated.*

At your window in Whitby, looking out over the ocean, at the fishing crews setting sail in the morning, and returning with full nets at night, and at the road that ran around the harbour, where, sometimes, people waited for the men to return from sea, you began to think about a new story. Whitby gave a rhythm and form to your own longings. You began to shape the restless yearning you had grown so accustomed to feeling over the past eighteen months into a plot.

Your heroine, Sylvia, is a vibrant, impulsive girl, who falls in love and becomes engaged to a rakish sailor called Charley. Her dull, religious cousin, Hepburn, who is also in love with her, witnesses Charley being captured by a press gang, but decides not to tell Sylvia, letting her believe that Charley has died. Mourning and alone, Sylvia agrees, reluctantly, to marry Hepburn, but all the while her love is alive, at sea, desperate to come home to her.

When, when are you coming to England dear Mr Norton? you wrote. You were standing at the shore, waiting for a ship to appear on the horizon. *I always look over the names of the American passengers, thinking you may have come.*

EG: *I have been hoping and hoping and wishing for letters from you.*

CEN: *Three years ago we met in Rome!*

EG: *The Campagna 'bits' in your letters always give one a sort of Heimweh.*

CEN: *For truly have you not made me feel at home with you, and how can one help desiring to know all home affairs & news?*

EG: *Yesterday . . . Meta and I were having a long, yearning talk about America, and our dear friends there. I am not sure that we did not shake hands upon a resolution that if we lived we would go over to America. I know we calculated time & expense, & knocked off Niagara, because we would rather see friends.*

CEN: *I am very glad that you are going to send me a photograph of yourself, and I shall thank you for it with warmest thanks if it be truly like you. I do not want to have to suit the truthful portrait in my memory to any unfamiliar look, and I would keep that image unchanged until the time when I may see you again.*

EG: *I think Rome grows almost more vivid in recollection as the time recedes. Only the other night I dreamed of a breakfast – not a past breakfast, but some mysterious breakfast which neither has been, nor, alas! would be – in the Via Sant'Isidoro dining room, with the amber sunlight streaming on the gold-grey Roman roofs and the Sabine hills on one side and the Vatican on the other. I sometimes think that I would almost rather never have been there than have this ache of yearning.*

2015

Sleep Study

I am registering with a doctor in Austin when I see the advert for the Sleep Study. It is printed on pink paper, and pinned to the noticeboard in the doctor's waiting room. The language is what catches my eye at first, glaring and familiar. It is written in the same, apparently universal, optimistic tone of the equivalents I saw in London: *Sad and struggling to sleep? Sad and sleeping soundly? Seeking volunteers with mild to moderate depression to participate in residential study. Volunteers will be awarded $1000 on successful completion of the study.* The bottom of the flyer has been cut into tabs, each printed with an email address. Two have already been torn off.

I go in to see a doctor, who tests my urine, confirms that I really do not have a UTI, and suggests I may have something called interstitial cystitis, which is like cystitis, except without the presence of any real infection, and therefore not really treatable.

'What causes it?' I say.

'We don't know.'

'Is that a way of saying it's in my head?'

'We don't know.'

'How do I get rid of it?' I say.

The doctor says I should stop taking vitamin tablets,

which I previously considered as my one truly healthy habit.

On the way out of the medical centre, almost without really deciding to, I tear off an email address from the bottom of the *Sad and Struggling to Sleep* poster.

The study will be carried out over a two-week period during which you will not leave the Sleep Centre. Prior to commencing partici-pation in the study, you will be interviewed by a researcher about your personal history of depression, as well as your sleep cycle and habits, to check you are eligible to participate. At this time, you will be assigned a subject number, by which you will be referred to for the duration of the study.

The sleep research unit is bunker-like and echoey. On the day of my screening appointment, I follow the doctor down a flight of stairs into a fluorescent-lit, controlled environment, where the walls are painted a disconcert-ingly dark shade of green. It feels a little like how I imagine a submarine to be. I sit on the edge of a bed to have my blood taken by a nurse who glares disapprov-ingly at my forearms and complains that I 'do not have good veins for cannulization'. The doctor, waiting by the door, makes a note of this. I watch my blood turn the syringe dark.

—

The residential session will take place in the Research Center's Sleep Unit. It will last fourteen days (three hundred and thirty-six hours). When you arrive at the unit your bag will be searched and any items not allowed e.g. medication, chewing gum, will be stored safely and returned to you on discharge. You will be asked to perform a breathalyzer test to ensure that you have not been drinking alcohol.

You will only be able to use your phone between 9 a.m. and 6 p.m. each day. Cell phones, watches and laptops will be collected by staff each evening and returned to you in the morning. You will sleep alone in an individual sleep cell. Your posture, meals and the lighting levels will be carefully controlled during the study.

In the doctor's office, he hands me an information pack, and then proceeds to read the whole thing out loud, word for word. I don't know where to look as he reads. There are no windows to gaze out of. For a while I follow along on the page as he describes procedures for checking into the unit that sound more like admission to prison than to a voluntary medical study. My mind begins to wander: I am in the midst of constructing a fantasy experiment in which Mrs Gaskell and William Wetmore Story and Harriet Hosmer are all inhabitants of the Sleep Unit, willing participants in my research, on hand to answer questions as I complete my thesis, when I hear the doctor mention that there can be no caffeine consumption for seven days prior to, and throughout, the study.

'Like, really none?' I ask.

'Absolutely none.'

'I will get such bad headaches,' I say.

The doctor looks as though he does not know what to do with this information, and then says, 'If that's true, you should probably consider cutting down in any case,' and continues to go over the other regulations: no anti-inflammatory drugs, no non-prescription drugs, no alcohol, no strenuous exercise.

He gives me a questionnaire to fill out – the kind with which I'm quite familiar, following the Body Study in my first year. In the past two weeks I have felt: *angry / peaceful / jittery / lonely / energetic / playful / hopeless / grouchy / composed.* I mark each emotion out of ten.

In the daytime, study participants are able to move freely between their individual sleep cells and the communal area. You are able to socialize with other participants. You are not allowed to leave the Sleep Unit. At 6 p.m. each evening, participants must return to their sleep cells. You will not leave your sleep cell until 9 a.m. the following day. On odd nights, you will sleep between 11 p.m. and 7 a.m., lying on your bed in darkness. On even nights, you will sit up in bed in dim light, and will remain awake. You will be awake from 7 a.m. until 11 p.m. the following day (forty continuous waking hours). On both odd and even nights, you will have electrodes attached to your head and a cannula (fine plastic tube) inserted into a forearm vein. We will measure your EEG (brain waves). Blood samples to be taken at regular intervals.

———

Of all the studies in which I have participated since the beginning of my Ph.D., this is the most extreme. I have never in my life stayed awake for forty hours straight, and I genuinely do not know if I have it in me to do it. It was all I could do to drink a glass of amino acid. It is, of course, also by far the best paid of all the studies I've seen, but now that I am no longer scrimping and saving to buy Eurostar tickets or transatlantic flights, perhaps it isn't necessary.

The doctor gives me a tour, showing me the communal area with sofas and a television, and then an 'individual sleep cell'. If the whole unit feels like a submarine, the sleep cell looks like the place they keep the missiles. It is a metal-walled box, with cameras in each corner of the ceiling pointed towards a narrow white mattress. The doctor shows me dials that control the temperature, light level and bed angle. There are small tubes trailing through the walls towards the bed. These, he says, connect to the cannula in the subject's arm, and allow for blood to be drawn from outside the cell without disturbing the subject if he or she is asleep. This, more than anything else, disturbs me. Sleep deprivation, living underground for two weeks, these things are challenges; an invisible person, on the other side of a metal wall, sucking blood from my sleeping body feels intimate, vampiric.

It is a relief, when the screening is over, to emerge out into the yellow Texas light. The world up at ground level is warm and bright and unsanitized and haphazard; cars pass by on the road and trees sway and when I get back to

Norma's house the chickens have escaped their coop and she is running around the yard trying to coax them back in.

A few days later, while I am in the reading rooms leafing through Elizabeth Barrett Browning letters, my phone buzzes. A librarian looks over, not exactly disapprovingly, but pointedly enough to make it clear that this should not happen again. I slide my phone onto my lap, silence it, and then open my inbox. There is an email from the Sleep Study researcher.

Dear Nell,

Thank you for your interest in participating in our research study on sleep disruption and depression. Unfortunately, following your screening appointment at the unit, you were found to be ineligible for the following reason(s):

Reason for non-inclusion of subject: depression is not present in the subject.

Thank you again for taking the time to attend the screening appointment.

I read the message through again, and have to repress the urge to laugh. It had not occurred to me, at least not in such unequivocal terms, that I might not be sad any more. Months have passed since I last sat in Dr Maier's office, overlooking Broadway, telling her about my grief. And when I think about my life since then – the move to

Austin, the treehouse, the comfortable wistfulness I feel reading the letters and notes left behind by William Wetmore Story and his friends – I realize that the researchers are right. Depression is not present in the subject.

2015

Great News

On the plane, I try to imagine how it will be. A few days away from the archives. A beach. Nice weather. Good food. I let my head fall against the window, where ice crystals are forming around the edges. We pass a pillar of cloud, its wisps reaching out like hands towards the aircraft's wing.

Max is in LA for a week, setting up meetings with agents and producers, touting a new script. He is renting an apartment, and has invited me to stay for a few days. Unlike my first visit to see him in Paris, there is no confusion about who will sleep where this time: there are two bedrooms. We are being very mature and organized. Max has saved up money in order to afford the trip, and has planned an itinerary of easy, pleasant activities for the time I'll be here. It will be a friendly visit, and that is all. Still, as he drives me back to his place from LAX, his right hand is lying on the armrest between us and instinctively I reach out and put mine over it. He doesn't react for a moment, then turns it palm up so he can lace his fingers through mine.

In Los Angeles, the light is thicker and yellower even than in Austin, and it clings to everything and makes everyone look attractive: Max, of course, and me, too, when I catch sight of my reflection in car windows and shopfronts. I feel light on my feet, and calm. Max wants to show me the whole city, which means spending a huge amount of time in the rental car, sitting in traffic on our way between Malibu beach and the Griffith Observatory and the Walt Disney Concert Hall. On each journey our hands find each other, and then, one evening, when we have had a few drinks and are walking arm in arm back towards the apartment after dinner, it feels natural, in-evitable even, that we should kiss, that we should hurry home, that we should spend the night in the same bed all over again. In the months before I got here I did a lot of thinking, a lot of reasoning with myself, about why my relationship with Max is really over, why it could never work, why its demise – so shocking at the time – had been inevitable from the start. But if this is a holiday from my work at the archives, could it not also be a holiday from worrying about all of that? I don't want to think any more.

Izra texts. 'So are you guys back together, or . . . ?' and I don't reply.

Louise: 'Please tell me you did not have sex with him.'

We take a train to Santa Barbara, the track skimming along the coast, all palm trees and blue sea and smooth, easy views. We join a vineyard tour, run by a small, intense Argentinian man called Tomas, who leads tastings in sev-eral wineries and tells us that 'the key to a good wine is the story behind it; you can taste if a wine was made with inspiration, with drama, with love.' I try my best, with each sip, to identify the drama and the love. The day passes in a haze, and Max and I can't stop touching each other and laughing at the kinds of jokes we used to make when we were together and Tomas says, 'I used to do a lot of bachelor, bachelorette parties, this kind of thing. Now I prefer to take smaller groups. I like the romantic couples. I like people who can taste the stories.' He beams at us and I feel oddly proud.

That evening, on the train back to the city, I can barely keep my eyes open. Max is dozing. I start to feel unwell. I have had too much to drink. There is a pain in my stomach, on the right-hand side, as though my insides are punishing me for the wine; they are writhing and twisting.

To distract myself, I look at my phone. Izra again: 'MAX UPDATE PLEASE. What is going on?' And a message from Alice, my brother's girlfriend: 'Hey! How are you? How's Texas? Do you want to speak on Skype?'

I close my eyes. The train thrums past the dark ocean.

The next morning, Max has booked a table for us to have brunch at a hotel near his apartment. We get dressed slowly, slightly hungover, and step out into the sunshine. Alice has messaged again: 'Hi! How are you? Are you free to Skype today?' I respond: 'I'm good! I'm in LA visiting a friend at the moment – shall we catch up next weekend?'

The walk from the apartment to the hotel takes us past mansions, gaudy and ornate, and as our heads begin to clear we play a game, choosing new homes for ourselves, new fantasy lives: I'll have this one, but I'd get rid of the fountains and plant more trees; I'll take this one, but change the pink front door.

'How much do these places cost?' I ask. 'Millions?'

'Millions and millions.'

'Oh, well, maybe when you sell the new screenplay,' I suggest, grinning, and then realize at once that this was the wrong thing to say. I have broken the unspoken rule that has, until now, been keeping this trip idyllic and sanguine: not to mention real life, not to revisit any of the factors that had contributed to our breakup, which included, but were not limited to: distance, money, uncertainty over Max's career and his writing.

'Maybe when I'm done with the archives in Austin, I could come to Boston for a few days,' I say, trying to change the subject. 'It could be fun. We could have dinner at Lineage. We could get the fish tacos.'

'That would be great,' says Max, and then a moment later, 'except that Lineage closed. It shut down a while ago.'

'Oh,' I say. 'Well, I guess we'll have to go somewhere else,' but already the idea feels duller, less plausible, and we finish the walk to brunch in silence.

At the hotel, there's a band playing jazz in the courtyard, and there are flowers everywhere, and vines swaying overhead, and at the table next to ours a chihuahua in a velvet coat with 'Beverley Hills' written across the back in diamanté is being fed pieces of ham by a blonde woman. My pocket buzzes with another text from Alice: 'It would be great to speak today, if possible.'

I put my phone face down on the table and wish she could have taken the hint. I'm busy. I'm with Max. A Skype chat with her and my brother sounds very nice, but it is the last thing I want to do today, when I am here in this glinting city and am determined not to think about anything. Then, I think how unlike her it is to be so pushy, that there must be something serious she needs to discuss. Surely, she wouldn't ignore my protestations that I'm too busy to speak, unless it were something serious.

'Do you mind if I call my brother quickly?' I say to Max. 'His girlfriend has been trying to get hold of me, and I think something might be wrong.'

'Sure,' he says, and I make the call.

The line is busy, and it is at this point that I start to panic. As Max orders drinks and food, my mind is turning over the scenarios that could possibly lead to Alice trying to contact me so urgently, and then being unavailable when I call. There must be something wrong with my brother, I think, otherwise he would tell me himself. But if something was wrong with my brother, then my parents would be the ones to let me know. So, it must be something wrong with my parents – both of them, otherwise the one who was fine would be in touch – and it must be something so awful that my brother is incapacitated with grief, leaving Alice to break the news of the disaster to me. By the end of thirty seconds' worrying, I have arrived at what feels like the only possible conclusion: my parents have died in a car crash.

My phone rings. It is Alice. Max reaches out to hold my hand across the table as I answer it.

'Hello?' I say. 'Alice? Are you OK? Is everything OK?'

'Hi,' she says. 'We're both here.'

'Hi,' I say.

My brother's voice: 'We've got some great news.'

'You have?'

'Yes,' he says. 'We've decided to get married.'

Somehow, I stammer my way through the rest of the conversation. I tell them both how pleased I am for them, and that I can't wait to hear all about their plans, and they say thank you and that they just wanted to be sure I heard it from them first, and we all agree that we will talk again soon, and then I hang up.

Afterwards, I know I should feel relieved, and the part of me that believed my parents were dead really is. More than that, though, I should feel pleased that my brother is happy. I stare at Max, who is watching me from across the table.

'They're getting married,' I say. 'They were just really excited to tell me.'

'Yeah,' says Max, 'I figured as much.'

'That's never going to be us, is it?' I say.

At the next table, the chihuahua has moved on to its second course, and is licking whipped cream from the blonde woman's fingers.

1862

A Woman Whom Everybody Loves

You were a swift writer, and didn't generally overthink things, and yet *Sylvia's Lovers* took you years. It wasn't like the anxiety-ridden diplomatic balancing act of writing Charlotte's biography, but more a kind of lethargy that crept into your life and slowed down your pen. You were tired. You were ill more often than you were healthy. The letters from Mr Norton, on which you had relied in previous years for energy and sustenance, became more and more irregular, with longer and longer periods of silence in between. You wondered often what he was doing, and heard about him from your mutual friends: he was settling in Boston, the Storys said, and had published a little book called *Notes of Travel and Study in Italy*.

Your own life, too, had moved on. Your girls were adults now, with dramas of their own, which you watched and supervised and counselled them over. In the quiet moments in between your other duties, you sat at your desk and pretended you were looking out to sea. You sent your mind back to Whitby, where your novel was set, and forced it to stay there as, gradually, painfully, your story developed word by word.

You were sitting that way one morning when a letter from America came, and despite yourself, after all the intervening years since you had last seen him, your heart fluttered when you saw who it was from. You set your pen down, and called to Hearn to bring you tea. A letter from Mr Norton was an event, and you wanted to savour it, to be perfectly comfortable, to settle yourself in readiness, as you would into a theatre seat before the curtain rose.

I am sure I may count upon your being glad with me when I tell you that I am very happy. I am engaged to be married to Miss Susan Sedgwick. – I wish that you knew her, for then you would wish me joy, and rejoice with me, with completest satisfaction . . . . She is a woman whom everybody loves.

For a long while, you sat, not reading the words but looking at their shape on the page. You were holding paper that Mr Norton himself had touched. You lifted it up to your nose and inhaled, searching for some residual trace of him. You fingered the edges of the sheets, and then traced the outline of the words: a woman whom everybody loves.

'Girls!' you called out. 'Girls!'

It was Meta who rushed in, waving her own letter. You saw the American stamps on it and knew that she, too, knew.

'Mama,' she said. 'Mr Norton is getting married!'

And you said, 'Yes, I know,' and realized that you were going to cry. Meta went to you and held you as though she was the parent and you the nervous, heartsick little girl. 'It's wonderful,' you said, your face pressed against her chest so that she couldn't see your eyes. 'I'm so happy for him.'

'I know you are, Mama,' said Meta. 'Of course you are. We all are.'

It should not have been a surprise. You should have known that in the increasingly long stretches of time between his letters to you, he would be establishing a life for himself in America. He was still young, and it was natural that he would want a wife, a family. After all, hadn't you wanted a husband? Hadn't you wanted children? And didn't you have those things? How could you be surprised that he had chosen the same for himself?

When you replied, you chose your words meticulously. You had never written anything more slowly, or with more care – not even the sections of *Sylvia's Lovers* that were finished, or the chapters that were still underway. 'I am so particularly glad to think of your being married,' you wrote, 'almost as if you were my own son.' You were pleased with this line. It was a clean re-casting of your relationship. It was a term you hoped would put his mind at rest about the impact his news might have had on you. Your interest in his affairs was strictly friendly, so asexual as to be, now, maternal.

'I have often thought,' you went on, 'that of all the men I ever knew you were not only the one to best appreciate women; but also (what is very probably) the other side of what I have just said, the one to require – along with your masculine friendships – the sympathetic companionship of a good, gracious woman.' A compliment and the very slightest rebuke, all bound up together. You had been the good, gracious woman whose sympathetic companionship Mr Norton had so needed, and he had appreciated you as no other man had. Now, you understood, you had been replaced. You asked for particulars. You wanted to know how they met, and where, and when, and what she looked like.

Later, a thick envelope arrived from Mr Norton's sister, Grace, providing all the details you had asked for, and you read it with a greedy, throbbing fascination, savouring every detail of *the woman whom everybody loves*. You sat at your desk, trying to formulate a reply, and after almost two hours, the page was blank, your pen still hovering uncertainly above it. What was there to be said about this description of Miss Susan, who was charitable and respectable and cheerful and lovely all at once? What could you say? You gave up trying to respond, and felt guilty about it every time your eye rested on Grace's letter amongst the other papers on your desk.

You could not be low and heartsick for long. Your novel needed an ending, and the news from Mr Norton prompted you to deliver it in a swift blow. The long-lost lover, Charley, returns from sea and begs Sylvia to marry him. She cannot; it is too late; she is married. She swears never to forgive her husband for keeping the truth from her, but neither can she abandon her marriage. And then, only a few months later, she learns that Charley has married an heiress, a babbling, shallow, pretty girl, whom everybody loves. It was, you said, the saddest story you ever wrote.

By the following year, you were ready to publish and you were ready, too, in your own way, to make peace. There were to be separate editions in America and in Britain, and you gave instructions for two different dedications to be printed. In the British version, it was to read, dutifully and understatedly,

This book
Is dedicated to
MY DEAR HUSBAND
By Her
Who Best Knows His Value

The American edition, you instructed, should read,

To all
My Northern Friends
With the truest sympathy of an
English Woman; and in an especial
manner to my dear Friend
Charles Eliot Norton
And to his Wife
Who, though personally unknown to me,
is yet dear to me for his sake.

2016

Tornado

It is Sunday morning, and in Austin, I have a Sunday morning routine. I wander through my neighbourhood to a little Italian cafe, where I meet Natalie, one of the other researchers at the Ransom Center, and a band plays gypsy jazz until noon. We sit out on the terrace in the sunlight, and read the news, and drink coffee, and I take the time to feel relieved that I do not have to give up caffeine, or stay awake for forty hours straight, and that my thesis is so nearly done. The end is truly in sight: I have three chapters, an introduction and the bare unfinished-but-nonetheless-promising bones of a conclusion.

On this Sunday morning, though, for possibly the first time since I moved to Austin, it is not sunny. The sky is a thick, mulchy grey, and there is an uneasy stillness in the air as I descend from the treehouse to make my way towards the cafe. Norma's wind charms are limp and silent. As I pass the front of the house, Norma waves at me through the window. I raise a hand in return, then realize she is gesturing at me to stop. Moments later, she appears at the front door.

'Where are you going?' she asks.

'To see a friend,' I say.

'But where?'

I tell her the name of her cafe, 'Dolce Vita,' and she shakes her head.

'Oh no,' she says, 'no, you can't go that far.'

'Why not?'

'You didn't hear?' she says. 'There's a tornado warning. You really shouldn't be going out at all.'

I retreat to the treehouse, text Natalie, and position myself at the window to watch as the cloudy weather reformulates itself into a fierce storm. It begins to rain so heavily that parts of the roof start to leak. The sound of the water smashing down overhead is thunderous; I can't even hear the wind chimes that are jangling frantically from the branches below me. It occurs to me that of all the places to be riding out a tornado, a treehouse is one of the least secure. Surely I'd have been safer at Dolce Vita.

Below in the yard, Norma appears in a bright pink mackintosh. I relax. She is coming to fetch me. She's going to let me wait out the storm in her house. But instead of moving towards the treehouse, she heads to the chicken coop and begins to move the birds inside, scooping them up one by one and carrying them under her arm. On seeing this I am certain: if the chicken coop is not strong enough to protect the chickens, the tree-house is not strong enough to protect me. I pack a plastic bag with my computer and a few library books, and then I make a run for it. I hurtle out of the door, down the wooden staircase and towards the shelter of Norma's back porch.

'Ah, yes,' she says, when she returns with the last chicken. 'I was just about to fetch you.'

I suppress a grumpy comment about her priorities, and follow her, dripping, down to the basement, where the chickens are clucking disconcertedly, pecking at the floor and shuffling between boxes of junk. Their clawed feet scrape along the concrete.

'How long do you think we'll be down here for?' I ask, but Norma just shrugs and says, 'Until the Lord's done ragin'.'

I sit on a box of old magazines, with my laptop on my knees, and work on my conclusion. Rome, I write, was exceptional. If anyone wondered, 'Why Rome?' at the beginning of my thesis, I am certain that, by the end, I've answered the question. There was nowhere else like it in the nineteenth century, no comparable meeting point where ideas and inspiration could move so freely between people of different nationalities, genders and sexualities. When Elizabeth Gaskell wrote that it was the 'tip-top point' of her life, it was because, in those three months she spent in Rome, she was free to communicate, to express herself as an artist and to receive ideas from others in a way that was impossible anywhere else.

I do not, in my thesis, write about love. I let it sit below the surface, as it did in the lives of my subjects, a heartbeat.

Hours later, water has begun to seep through the ceiling on the far side of the space. I point this out to Norma, who nods and says, 'Just so long as it's water coming down, and not the house going up, we're all right.' Just then, the pain in my right side that began in LA returns, a twisting, wrenching sharpness, and I have to bend over my knees and take deep breaths to stop myself from yelling. I pant through it, waiting for it to pass, and trying to distract myself by reading and re-reading the words I've just written. Norma notices me crouching and staring, bemused, at my computer screen, and says, 'You'll make yourself crazy, tapping away at that damn machine all day. You should look at something else for a change.' I'm about to gasp a reply when, as suddenly as the pain came on, it subsides.

I feel as though I have woken up. I am disoriented. The chickens have settled, huddled together near my feet; in the corner of the room, water is still dripping from the ceiling, amassing in a black puddle. I turn to my computer. I look at thesis.docx, and discover that I have finished. I have reached the end. It brings me up short.

When Gaskell dreamed of America, did it look like Rome, as is given in A. V. Chapple and Arthur Pollard's *The Letters of Mrs. Gaskell* (1997), or like home, as in Jane Whitehill's *Letters of Mrs. Gaskell and Charles Eliot Norton* (1932)? This divergence of readings of the same word is symptomatic of the link between the three places evoked here and in Gaskell's other writing: Rome was home, and America, defined by her relationship with Charles Eliot Norton, was therefore like both Rome, and home. Rome was where Gaskell was free to encounter new art, and other artists, to forge her own relationships and to tell her own stories. It was a city through which she saw new worlds.

Norma scatters grain on the floor at her feet, and the chickens strut towards her, clucking. The cursor blinks after the final word, 'worlds', on my screen. Below it, the word-count is bulging; I've reached the limit. There's still a strange feeling in my side where the pain was, a dull echo, but for now, all I can think is that I'm finished. The Americans Mrs Gaskell met in Rome have been researched, their works and ideas recorded. My own American, who is back in Boston, has been visited, kissed and given up. It is time for me to go home.

1878

William's Party

Mr William Wetmore Story decided to throw a party. It had been years since he'd last done so, since his apartment at the Palazzo Barberini had been noisy with the voices of guests, and with music, and with laughter. He had been back to America over the summer, accompanied by his son Waldo, to give a series of lectures on the subject 'What is the Use of Art?'. He had toured town halls, artists' institutes, small cities, had met Americans of every description – educated, uneducated, rich, poor, curious, incurious – and all of them had seemed foreign to him, citizens of a country that was no longer his own. He did not recognize America, with its railways and factories and strange smells. Even the voices seemed different, the accents more distinctive. Waldo was even more lost than he, staring bemusedly at the place that was, purportedly, his homeland. He was twenty-three years old and had never lived there. Father and son were both strangers in America.

When they reached Rome, he felt a surging joy to be home, to be surrounded once again by people he loved, who understood him, amongst whom he had lived for thirty years. So, he began to plan a party. That autumn he would celebrate the thirtieth anniversary of his arrival in the city. He would gather his old friends together again. Robert Browning was back in Italy for the first time in seventeen years; he had left when his wife died, and William had seen him in London sometimes, but never, since then, in Rome. Mr Gibson was dead now. Mr Powers was dead. Mr Hawthorne, too. Miss Hosmer was still there, more eccentric than ever, though Miss Stebbins had run off to America with Miss Cushman, and Miss Cushman had died of pneumonia. Miss Hosmer was less sprightly, more reserved, and had turned her attention away from art and towards mechanical invention: she was working on a perpetual motion machine and had patented several designs. She had collected another member to what William had taken to calling her 'Harem (scarem)' of lady sculptors, a Miss Edmonia Lewis, who worked at her marble harder than anyone.

He had been sour, bad company to his artist friends in recent years. He had watched them applaud each other and become famous, had read profiles of them in journals, and couldn't help feeling embittered. It was true that his talents, too, had been recognized, but it felt as though the attention he received was too little, too late, considering the years he had worked, the contribution he had made. It did not please him the way he had thought it would, the way it seemed to please those around him. He had written all those books of poetry. He had created all those statues, which clustered in his studio like a theatre audience awaiting curtain-up. And yet all people wanted to see or talk about was his *Cleopatra*, because that was the statue Hawthorne had described in *The Marble Faun*. Was it really true that his greatest claim to fame would be his role in that blasted novel? Was he, William Story, to be remembered more for Hawthorne's work than his own? He had been irritable and resentful, even to Robert; he had published a snide poem in the *Atlantic*, complaining of ill-treatment by his critics and peers, venting his disillusionment.

Fame seemed, when out of reach, how sweet and grand!
How worthless, now I grasp it in my hand!

Give me the old enthusiasms back,
Give me the ardent longings that I lack, –
The glorious dreams that fooled me in my youth,
The sweet mirage that lured me on its track, –
And take away the bitter, barren truth.

What matters now the lauding of your lips,
What matters now the laurel wreath you plait
For these bald brows, for these gray hairs? It slips
Over my eyes and helps to hide my tears.
I am too old for joys – almost for fears.

Now, restored in the Palazzo Barberini after his American tour, he saw that it had been wrong of him. His friends had always looked to him for fun, for gaiety, for the continuity of dear old Rome the way they had always known it. He should not, now, let them down. It was not their fault that he was miserable. It was not their fault that they were praised more warmly than he was by the press, that they were happier. He would throw a party, and everyone would come, and he would be at the centre of everything again.

The courtyard of the Palazzo Barberini was glowing; lamps lined the driveway and encircled the fountain. On each stone step that led to the Storys' apartment was a candle, flickering, illuminating separate spheres of ancient stone on the way up. Inside, William's daughter, Edith, was sitting near the door, bouncing her baby on her knee, ready to greet guests. William himself roamed uneasily from room to room, checking everything was in order, the piano tuned, the wine ready, his most well-loved statues correctly positioned to receive the best light, until Emelyn snapped at him to sit down and let her worry about it. He went then to the window, and watched the first carriage arrive; young friends of Waldo emerged, their faces golden in the lamplight, laughing and excited as they crossed the courtyard to the staircase. Moments later he heard them enter the apartment, Edith's welcome, Waldo's greeting, the noises of general cheer, of a party beginning. More carriages were drawing up; there was a line of them at the gates, and in the parlour somebody began to play the piano. He felt something lift from his chest, a kind of giddiness beginning in his groin, his stomach, and he began to beam.

As the rooms filled and the volume of their combined conversations rose, William moved between circles, sampling and moving on, lifting titbits from one to drop into another. There were murmurings about Auguste Rodin, a

French sculptor who had been in Italy a few years before, but was now in Paris, showing a work entitled *The Age of Bronze*.

'There is something new in it,' Miss Lewis said. 'It is so entirely true to life, and yet, unlike anything ever seen before.'

'It's a low type of art,' countered William, who had seen a photograph of the statue in the newspaper. 'The fellow has talent, but will never come to much unless he elevates his mind. There is so little to be gained in mere expressiveness. He wants a nobler subject.'

Another group was discussing a new story by Henry James entitled *Daisy Miller*, which had appeared that summer in the *Cornhill Magazine*.

'It is not so brilliant as *Roderick Hudson*,' said a young woman, a friend of Edith. 'I did not see that she really had to die at the end.'

'Oh, she absolutely had to die,' said Edith, looking wry. 'We could not possibly allow such an improper young lady to go unpunished.'

'For goodness' sake, you have both spoiled the ending,' said Miss Hosmer. 'I have only just reached the part where they get to Rome.' She looked away for a moment, and her expression softened. 'Oh, look,' she said. 'Mr Browning has come.' And there, on the other side of the room, was William's old friend, aged, but not beyond recognition, striding towards them and reaching out a hand to shake his.

'Here you are,' said Robert. 'Here you still are.'

'Here we still are,' said William. 'All of us who are left.'

Miss Hosmer took Robert's hand and murmured, 'Ah, I've missed this ugly paw,' and then the three of them stood, looking about them, saying nothing for a long while.

William thought of breaking their silence with something along the lines of, 'It's just like old times,' but in truth it was not like the old times. There were too many absent friends, too many who had left or died, and they who remained were too old to dance, or to put on the plays they once had performed. The younger generation was singing now.

When the last guest had left, William stared at the apartment, empty, silent, Emelyn dozing in a chair by the fire. Edith and her husband had already gone to bed. Waldo was smoking at the window, looking down at the courtyard where the servants were extinguishing lamps. The fountain folded over and over itself, glittering until the last light went out.

'Did you have a good time, Father?' said Waldo, turning.

Beside him, William looked out at the dark, ruined city, and put a hand on his son's shoulder. 'For years and years,' he said.

2016

Accoutrements of womanhood: three observations

One: An Engagement Ring

I see them on the tube, these women. My eyes slide to the fourth fingers of their left hands, where diamonds sit against their skin, leering at me as they catch the light. I try to imagine their lives, which seem, from the safe distance of the other side of the carriage, somehow defined by this thing they have decided to do. I know nothing else about them. They are going to get married. That is all. They are the heroines of their own love stories. Nothing has gone wrong for them yet.

Depending on my mood, my own unchosen, undecorated hands seem either childish and embarrassing, or brave, alternative, independent, as I fold and unfold them in my lap.

Two: A Baby on Board

When the woman has collected not only her engagement ring, but also, next level up, the secondary gold band, she is ready to have a 'Baby on Board' badge pinned to the lapel of her coat. For this, she is either awarded a seat on the tube, or a wall of eyes turned the other way, pretending not to have noticed her.

Even more than I stare at diamond rings, I stare at the rounded stomachs of pregnant women.

I have reached a state of more-or-less relaxed ambivalence about marriage. I am embarrassed and annoyed by its excesses and its smugness, envious of its securities. But children, the possibility, pros and cons of them, preoccupy me. If Max and I had stuck to our original timeline, we'd be living together in the same country and the idea of creating a new human would not seem as distant, outlandish, impossible, as it does to me now.

I am thirty. I am single. I am no longer heartbroken, but still, the idea of being with someone who is not Max feels impossible. The idea of being with someone who is Max is clearly impossible. I order an information pack from a sperm bank and when it arrives in the post, I leaf through it over a glass of wine and try to imagine what it would be like to have a child without the help of someone else.

I ask my mother about it. 'Aren't you worried that it will affect your writing?' she says. 'I'm not sure you'd be able to write, with a baby to care for.'

This does not seem positive, but it is also, I hope, not necessarily true. I turn to Louise for a second opinion. She is nine months pregnant, large, uncomfortable and very ready to discuss children with me. 'Would you have the baby if you weren't with Frank?' I ask. 'Would you have the baby by yourself?'

She pauses to think about it, stroking her stomach as though, like a crystal ball, it might reveal the answer. 'You know, I really don't think I would,' she says after a while, and then, seeing that I am crestfallen, 'but that doesn't mean you shouldn't. Maybe it would be fine.'

Three: A Baby

On the day I am due to submit my completed Ph.D. thesis, the pain in my right side returns so intensely that I can't move. I kneel on all fours on the floor and rock back and forth and breathe noisily as though I'm in labour. In a panic, I call Louise, who arrives with her new-born son, Zachary, in a sling and administers painkillers to me. Later, when I am calmer, she puts the baby next to the two bound copies of my thesis, takes a photo and sends it to Izra and Holly with the caption 'some of the things we made this year'. Then she takes the thesis to the exams office at King's on my behalf.

By the time she texts to reassure me that she got it in on time, the pain has vanished again. 'I didn't tell them I wasn't you. I just handed it over with the paperwork. They said congratulations on finishing,' she writes, 'especially with a new baby.'

2016

Critic

Two months after Louise and Zach submitted my thesis on my behalf, and two weeks before my viva is due to take place, the pain in my right side returns yet again. There was a brief respite when things seemed to be getting better; I still needed to pee all the time, and my back had started aching, which I attributed to carrying an increasingly heavy Zach around, but at least the pain was gone. Then, one Saturday morning at 4 a.m., I wake myself up screaming.

I try to reposition myself in the bed, to find a way of lying that lessens the pain. I take paracetamol, and then ibuprofen, and then aspirin. Still, it feels as though something is breaking inside me, and I can't keep myself from yelling with each exhale. I am back on the floor, rocking like a disturbed zoo animal, and when I call my parents to ask for advice, I have to explain what is going on in short bursts, between howls.

'I think you need to go to hospital,' my mother says, at which point it seems very obvious that I do. I call the out-of-hours doctor, who listens to my alternating whimperings and shrieks, and sends an ambulance.

I am still in my pyjamas, and in the half-hour before the paramedics arrive, I undertake what, in my current state, is a colossal challenge: I put on a bra. Every stage of this process is excruciating and I stop at several points to retch: lifting my top over my head to take it off; reaching up to my underwear drawer; sliding my arms through the straps; twisting my hands behind my back to hook the clasp. By the time my doorbell rings, I am half delirious with pain and have thrown up on my bedroom floor, but I am, triumphantly, wearing underwear.

I am strapped to a trolley and loaded into an ambulance, still yelling so loudly that my neighbours come to their windows and stare. My last glimpse of the street as the doors close behind me is of curious, craning faces. Once we set off, the paramedics give me small doses of morphine, which don't stop the pain, but dim it for a few minutes at a time. We arrive at King's College Hospital. A brief glimpse of the sky overhead as I'm wheeled inside. A corridor. Suddenly the paramedics aren't here any more, and the painkillers have worn off, and I am yelling again, and someone says, 'Who is dealing with this?' A small white room. A nurse asking me what I've taken. I say I don't know. I give her my arm and she swabs it with alcohol: cold, rough against my skin. A needle.

'I'm giving you morphine, OK?' she says.

'A lot?' I ask.

'A lot,' she says, and already I can feel it taking effect, wrapping itself around me like insulation. I can still feel the pain, but I am detached from it, far away from myself – from the self that is lying on the trolley in the white room, no longer yelling but whimpering and mumbling at the ceiling. I lose any sense of time, and instead I am content to exist in my morphine-dream, in which a person like me is in pain, a person for whom I have a great deal of sympathy, but who is separate and beyond my control.

At some point, a doctor arrives, and prods my stomach, and asks me to rate the pain out of ten.

'It is a ten when I am there,' I say.

'When you're there?'

'I'm not there right now.'

'OK.'

Later, a doctor appears with a medical student. 'We're just going to take a look at your tummy. Is that all right?' She directs the young man to examine me.

He is nervous and uncertain. 'Should I expose the patient?' he says, to her, and she says, 'Well, ask the patient.'

'May I expose you now?' he says, and I agree contentedly to let him lift my shirt up, because I am not there, and in any case, I am wearing a bra underneath it. His cold fingers prod my ribs, my diaphragm and then hit the site of the pain. For a brief moment, I come back to myself enough to yell. 'Does that hurt?' he asks. 'How much out of ten?'

Later still, my father is there, staring into my pupils. I tell him I've had morphine and he says, 'Yes, I can see you have.'

I fall asleep, and when I am next awake I hear my father talking to a man. 'There are no beds,' the man is

251

saying. And at some point even later – my father says it is still Saturday – I am wheeled on my trolley into a lift, and then along some corridors, and then into a small room, past another woman on another trolley, and left there.

'We think it's your appendix,' a doctor says, 'but we need to send you for a scan. When was the last time you ate?' he asks.

'Yesterday,' I say.

'And drank?'

'This morning.'

'OK,' he says. 'We'll have your scan done, and then get you into surgery as soon as we can.'

But the scan is not done. Someone arrives and reports that it cannot be done at the weekend; there is nobody who will do it. I hear a whispered, irritated conversation between two voices on the other side of a curtain.

'We have to operate without the scan.'

'We can't operate without the scan.'

I lie on the trolley for three days. They are always just about to operate, which means I can't have food or drink, but then, at the last minute, there is always a reason why they can't. At one point on the Sunday evening, they decide they really are about to take me to theatre and just need to do some blood tests before I go, but discover somebody forgot to replace my drip that morning, and I am so dehydrated that the doctor can't find a vein.

By Monday, I am unsure where I am. My parents and

friends have come in and out, and each time I open my eyes I am not sure who will be there. It is for this reason that when I look up to see Mrs Gaskell perched at the end of my trolley, I am not really surprised. She is one of many visitors, real or otherwise.

'Mrs Gaskell?' I say.

'Look at you,' she says. 'Just look at you. What a state.'

'You really need to work on your trolleyside manner,' I say.

'And you really need to brush your hair.'

'I wrote about you,' I tell her. 'I wrote all about you in Rome.'

Her face softens then, and she says, as I knew she would, because, of course, she is in my head and I am making it all up, *It was the tip-top point of my life.*

When I come round from the surgery I am shivering. I can't stop. My teeth are chattering and I am shaking so hard that the side of the trolley is jangling against the drip stand. A nurse brings a tube that blows hot air under the covers, and it feels almost like having the morphine again: a cocooning relief. I let my head fall back. Gradually, the trembling subsides.

'Did it go OK?' I ask the woman who is standing by my pillow. 'Did they take out my appendix?'

'The doctor will come and speak to you soon,' she says, and I know at once that something is wrong, from the way she won't meet my eye, from the way she doesn't say, as I overhear someone telling the patient on the other side of the curtain, 'Everything went well. It was all fine.'

'What happened?' I ask. 'Please can you tell me what happened?'

I wait all night and half of the next day to find out. Then a consultant comes round with my file, and explains that the cause of the pain was not, in fact, my appendix, but my right ovary, which had swollen to the size of a grapefruit and twisted five times on the fallopian tube.

'Have you noticed any other symptoms recently? Frequent urination? Back pain?'

'Yes,' I say. 'Yes, both of those things.'

'That's fairly typical if you have an ovary the size of a grapefruit,' she says.

There seems to me nothing typical at all about having an ovary the size of a grapefruit. 'How do we fix it?' I ask. 'What happens now?'

'We had to take it out,' the consultant says. 'It was dead. It was gangrenous. There was no viable tissue left.'

'You took out my ovary?'

I think I might cry – I want to cry – but at that moment, my entire torso seizes up with pain and all I can do is lie there, paralysed, trying not to breathe. This 'discomfort', the doctor says, is normal after the kind of surgery I've had, and will pass. I wait. She waits. And then it does pass, and the tears come.

'I still have one left?' I ask, and she says, yes, I do, and that as far as they know it is healthy, but that, because I have all my eggs in one basket, it would be wise to consider, as a matter of some urgency, my 'fertility options'.

'A grapefruit,' I tell Mrs Gaskell, who is back, standing beside my trolley, close enough this time that I can really scrutinize her. 'A grapefruit. I did not see that coming.'

'Nor did I,' she says.

Everything about her is strange: her clothes, the cut of them and the way they sit around her body; the shape of her waist and bust, sculpted with stays; the way she smells, musty and sweat-tinged.

'I must seem so bizarre to you,' I say.

'Yes,' she says, casting her eyes over the hair I already know she finds unacceptably messy, over the hospital gown, which is still blood-stained from the surgery; nobody has come to change it yet.

'I'm a single woman with a single ovary,' I tell her. 'I'm thirty years old. I have to consider my fertility options as a matter of some urgency.'

'I see.'

'Max is gone. My right ovary is gone. Should I just have a baby by myself, Mrs Gaskell? Is that the right thing to do?'

'*I think an unmarried life may be to the full as happy, in process of time, but I think there is a time of trial to be gone through with women, who naturally yearn after children,*' says Mrs Gaskell. I have heard this from her before, in a letter to Charles Eliot Norton.

'That's not true any more, though,' I tell her. 'Unmarried doesn't have to mean childless. What I'm saying is, should I do this alone? Should I use a sperm donor, and have a baby, alone?'

There is no way Mrs Gaskell can comprehend the question I am asking. From where she sits, beside my trolley, and yet still, somehow, deep inside the nineteenth century, there is no such thing as sperm donation, there is no such thing as a baby without a man.

My gynaecological situation, it occurs to me now, is a perfect metaphor for my position on reproduction. Half of me, the left ovary, is primed and ready to go: I want to have a baby; I have always imagined that I would eventually be a mother, although until recently I have also assumed that Max would be part of the process; I am ready, nonetheless, for that 'eventually' to be now. The other half of me, the right ovary, is a twisted, agitated mess that has contemplated the same questions – motherhood, single or otherwise – and reached a different conclusion; has not yet adjusted to the breakup, or the recalibration of my future that it prompted; is convinced that having a baby alone will mean the end of my career; is in pain.

Perhaps I have said all this aloud, because Mrs Gaskell murmurs, 'The right ovary isn't there any more. The right ovary died. It's gone.'

The right ovary is gone.

'What would you do, Mrs Gaskell? If you were doing it all over again, would you marry Mr Gaskell, and have children? Would you do it, looking back, knowing what you know now?'

She sits down in the chair by the window, and folds her hands in her lap. 'All I wanted was to tell stories,' she says. 'I was a writer. I would have been a writer no matter what had happened, Mr Gaskell or not, Marianne or not, Meta or not. It was as unchangeable as any solid fact – as unchangeable as Mr Gaskell's hatred of foreign food, as unchangeable as factory smoke over Plymouth Grove, as unchangeable as a dead ovary.'

'Yes, I can see that.'

'That is not true for everyone, of course. There are countless women who would have written if their lives had only been different: if there had not been a man, or if there had not been a baby.'

'Yes.'

'But you have a hand in all of this. You have a choice to make, true, but once you have made it, there are more choices still: how you will act, how you will write, and when. What I meant to suggest is that you can address these questions as the author of your experiences, rather than just the critic.'

The word she alights on, so out of place in the fluorescent-lit, sanitized hospital room – *critic* – makes me half sit up in bed, only to discover that post-surgery this is not a movement I can easily make. I yelp with pain.

'What's the matter?' she says.

'Mrs Gaskell!' I say. 'I have to leave the hospital!'

'Whatever for?'

'My viva! My viva is next week. I have to go home and prepare. I have to be ready to answer questions about you.'

2016

Viva

'The viva voce,' reads the King's website, '(literally: live voice, or by the living voice) is an oral examination whereby your Ph.D. work is examined by two examiners, usually specialists in the field.' By my living voice, I will defend my thesis against the attacks of an art historian who has published a book on the relationship between contagious diseases and artistic influence in nineteenth-century Rome, and a Romanticist who specializes in female travellers in Italy.

'Are you sure you want to do this?' asks Joyce, when I call her to let her know I've been in hospital. 'We can postpone.'

'No,' I say, 'I want to get it done. I need it to be done.'

Much as I'm dreading my viva, I'm appalled by the idea that it could be cancelled at the last minute. The three years of labour, anxiety and anticipation I spent working on my Ph.D. are irrevocably bound up in my mind with my relationship with Max. I am desperate to move on from my stultifying days in the library, and equally desperate to move on from him. So, the week after I am discharged from hospital, I shuffle into the Virginia Woolf building, into the same office where, eighteen months previously, I had my upgrade interview, and submit to another round of questioning.

'We understand you haven't been well,' says the Romanticist, as I take my seat.

This gives me hope that my examiners will take pity on me, and go easy on my work. In this, and in many other things, which I wrote in my thesis, I am rapidly proved incorrect.

Issues my examiners have with my research:

— Inadequate justification for choice of subjects: why have I chosen to write about Gaskell, Hosmer, Browning, Barrett Browning, Hawthorne, Story and not, say, Powers, Akers, Landor?
— Inadequate justification for choice of timeframe: what is significant about the mid-century as opposed to, say, the first half? Why does it tail off so vaguely in the 1890s?
— Inadequate demonstration that Rome was different to other sites of artistic collaboration in Italy. And why, in a thesis that claims to be about Rome, is there a peculiar and irrelevant section towards the end about Rodin and modernist sculpture in Paris?
— Inadequate critical distinction between fiction and non-fiction sources.
— There are some strange, misplaced commas in my bibliography.

———

259

I listen to their complaints, and tell them why I think they are wrong, although I do not say what I believe to be the correct answer to most of their questions, with the exception of the comma issue: 'Mrs Gaskell.' I have chosen to write about Mrs Gaskell, and the people she knew and met in Rome. I have chosen to write about the mid-century because that is when Mrs Gaskell was there. I have focused on Rome because Mrs Gaskell was focused on Rome. It was the tip-top point of her life. Right at the beginning of this process, three years ago, I picked a subject, and that subject, it became clear, was Mrs Gaskell.

The examiners do not seem pleased. I am not putting up a particularly good fight; I'm still on a lot of pain-killers and my jeans, as I sit at the table, are digging into the incision in my stomach through which my ovary was removed: a zig-zag that descends from my belly button.

The hands on the clock on Joyce's shelf have leapt forward since I last looked. We have been doing this for nearly two hours, this back-and-forth of aggressive question and defensive answer. I realize that it is not going well, that they don't like the thesis, that three years of work, and all that time I spent with Mrs Gaskell – the days in the Rare Books Reading Room at the British Library, at Columbia, at the Harry Ransom Center – were wasted. Those reasons I gave Max as we wandered through the Louvre (a Ph.D. will help my writing; a Ph.D. will help me get a job; a Ph.D. will mean I'm an expert in something); none of them will mean much if, at the end of the process, I don't actually get my Ph.D.

'I think we'll leave it there,' says the Romanticist, and then, suddenly, it is over, and they have left the room.

They haven't told me the outcome, which I expected they would do at the end. I sit at the table for a moment, letting it sink in: they haven't told me the outcome because they consider it perfectly obvious, from the issues they have raised and the tenor of the interrogation, that I have failed. I have failed.

I push myself up to a standing position, a slow and painful process, and limp to the bathroom, where I lock myself in a cubicle to cry. I can't face Joyce, or the other Ph.D. students, who will be waiting in the graduate student lounge, anxious to hear what happened, what I was asked, what it was like. I wish Mrs Gaskell would come to me again, but I'm not nearly spaced out or drugged up enough to summon her, and instead I sit on the toilet and confront the fact that I have let her down.

My phone buzzes in my bag. I don't want to look at it. My parents, brother, friends, are waiting to hear how the viva went, and I am going to have to tell them that I failed.

It's a text message from Joyce: 'Congratulations! Can't find you to tell you in person, but you passed. Apparently the examiners forgot to let you know?'

1865

Mortis

Two things happened after you died.

First: Meta wrote to Mr Norton, clarifying, not that clarification was required, that you had always loved him. 'She was so faithful to you – so unswerving in her affection, not only to you, but to all that she had known through you; in her [. . .] longing for freedom and right to triumph in her "dear America".'

Second: Mr Norton's daughter was born and named after you. You never reached America, but Elizabeth Gaskell Norton was a true child of the New World. She grew up in a big wooden house called Shady Hill in Cambridge, Massachusetts, and spent her summers in Ashfield, roaming the dark American forests you dreamt of. Like her father, like you, she grew up to have famous friends: Henry James, Edith Wharton, Rudyard Kipling.

I was going to write, 'It never occurred to you that you were going to die.' I was going to point out how busy you were, writing your new novel, *Wives and Daughters*, which was being serialized in the *Cornhill Magazine*. You were in the middle of purchasing and renovating a house in Hampshire called The Lawn, which you did without Mr Gaskell's knowledge or sanction. He wouldn't approve, so you planned to present it to him as a fait accompli: it was a way of forcing departure from Manchester after more than thirty years of barely tolerating your residence in the city.

You wrote to Mr Norton to tell him about it: 'I did a "terribly grand thing"! and a secret thing too! only you are in America and can't tell. I bought a house and 4 acres of land'. It was bullish and deliberate of you, using your own money for your own ends; you lived to the last at the very boundaries of what was acceptable within the kind of marriage people did not gossip about.

You were busy looking forward, but it's possible this was because you were looking beyond yourself, your own lifetime. The Lawn would be a home for your unmarried daughters after you were gone – would provide the security that enabled Meta to paint, and to become a mountaineer, and never need a husband to provide for her. You were busy looking forward because your mind, increasingly, dragged you back. Your perpetual nostalgia had become chronic over the past year.

Perhaps, after all, in the midst of your projects and plans, it *had* occurred to you that you were going to die. The last letter you wrote to Mr Norton seems so self-consciously a *last letter*, but it's possible I only read it that way because I can see there are no more pages in the book, that after your sign-off on that final note – 'with dear love to you all believe me ever your true and affectionate friend, E. C. Gaskell' – is the back cover, red and fraying.

Sometimes I dream I go over to Boston and see you and Susan and the little ones. But I always pass into such a cold thick damp fog, on leaving the river at Liverpool that I never get over to you. But my heart does; and I send my dear dear love.

Those were very happy Roman days – I have loved America ever since.

But life never flows back, – we shall never again have the old happy days in Rome, shall we?

In the absence of touch, taste, smell, sound, all you shared with Mr Norton were memories and words. Across the Atlantic, you wrote to each other, you read each other from afar, and still, sometimes words failed. When Mr Norton read *Sylvia's Lovers*, along with its American dedication, he sent you a letter of praise. But even then there was a gap in his writing, in place of what he meant to say. Words, he wrote, were insufficient:

> Since I last wrote to you, I have read *Sylvia's Lovers*. Had I taken up the book by chance, not knowing who wrote it, I should have read it with deep interest, – and with tender, respectful admiration. But having had the happiness of knowing & loving you, and you

having given me the book in a way that makes it very dear to me, – I have read it with such feeling as few other books have ever called out in me. It is impossible for me to say what I should like to say, – for the words do not convey when written the true impression of feeling.

There was so much you could not say. There was so much you said indirectly. There was so much you said directly, which is now lost, the paper burned, disintegrated, torn, and which I will never read.

In the *Anglistica & Americana* book of your letters that Max gave me, there is a fragment of a letter from Mr Norton to you. He is talking about evolutionary biology, about the phenomenal scientific discoveries of the nineteenth century ('At any rate, I wait to be convinced that I am nothing but a modified fish!'), and how what had been discovered by contemporary scientists was a tiny fraction of the truth. 'How little they know compared with what might be known!' he wrote. And then, 'It seems as'.

There, the line stops. The editor has added a note: '[the ending to this letter is lost].' The ending to this letter is lost. How little they know compared with what might be known. The ending to this letter is lost.

When did you lose it, Mrs Gaskell? Or perhaps it wasn't you who mislaid it. Perhaps it was Meta, tidying your papers, neglecting to pick up the last page. How little I know compared with what might be known.

—

You took your girls to see The Lawn, gathering them around you as you always did, showing them the grounds, the rooms that would be theirs, the new furniture you had bought and the study where you would finish *Wives and Daughters*. You were full of talk and stories, and of all the possible things to be discussing when, mid-sentence, you gasped and died, you were talking about Rome. Letters sent by your friends after your death dwell on this fact, on the name of the city being your last word on earth.

It is so absolutely like you as to seem implausible, that you keeled over mid-flow, full-throttle, with that word on your lips.

I wish we could see you again, Mr Norton; we never thought it would be so long, did we, when we parted?

2017

Three Types of Ending for this Book

When I started writing *Mrs Gaskell and Me*, I did not know how it would end. I was hurt, still, by Max, and the way things went. I was still, on occasion, angry. I had conversations with people about the forced, unnatural nature of the traditional narrative ending. It's like trying to tie up the loose ends of an octopus, I complained. Nothing is ever over, I said. Nothing is ever done. My life does not stop because the book ends. How am I supposed to contrive an ending to an ongoing situation?

Ending One: In which I do the thing I almost did when Max and I first broke up, and get on a plane to Boston. It is snowing, because it is always snowing in my imagined version of Boston, but not with the kind of oppressive, metaphysical snow that made Max feel trapped and overwhelmed; it will be a light, gleaming dusting that makes everything look picturesque. I send a text to Max and say, 'Come to Lineage, right now' (because, in this version, the restaurant has not closed down).

I am already there, at our old table in the window, and before he arrives I order all the food we used to love, the tacos, the brioche rolls, the wine he likes. When Max arrives outside he sees me through the window, and pauses, looking in. His face is stricken, that old familiar petrified look, and I wave and gesture at him to come in, *it's freezing out there*.

Inside, he sits at the table, and his jacket is flecked with unmelted snow, and I say, 'The reasons to be apart aren't as good as the reasons not to be. Come on. Let's get married,' and he says, 'OK.'

We'll have a wedding, the way our friends and siblings have had weddings, and maybe after that we'll be happy, or we won't.

The second ending takes place many years in the future, when I am in LA, or New York, or Boston, and am more sophisticated than I am now, having learned the sorts of lessons one surely learns in one's thirties and put them into practice with aplomb. I know exactly what to do with my hair, and the length to wear it that is not so short as to seem severe, but not so long as to seem unruly. I have an acute understanding of the shades of lipstick that work best with my complexion. I am definitely wearing sunglasses. I am probably wearing a hat.

I have been doing something urbane and worldly, and as I come out of the place where I was doing it, I see, across the street, Max. He is sitting on a bench, reading *The End of the Affair*, and in surprise I call out.

'Max!' I shout. 'Max!' He looks up and freezes, and everything that has happened between us seems momentarily visible on his face. Then he crosses over to me, and kisses me on the cheek.

'It's good to see you,' I say.

'How's John?' he asks.

(In this version, I have married and recently divorced a politician or a millionaire or a film producer called John, and have several charming and well-provided-for children.)

'Oh,' I say, 'John? I wouldn't know.'

Max's gaze meets mine for a second.

He says, 'Do you have time for a coffee?' and either I do, or I don't.

The third ending happens in the hospital, as I lie on my trolley in the gynaecology ward after my operation, staring at a wall I will forever remember for some reason as pale blue, though my friends correct me and say it was white. I peel back the dressing to inspect the surgical wounds on my stomach. The skin is bulging where the seam is, with wisps of stitches poking through like the legs of an insect trying to escape. My belly button is unrecognizable. I expand my habit of metaphorical navel-gazing to include literal navel-gazing. There is a sense of finality in this: an end of something.

I have one less body part today than I had yesterday. Somewhere else in the building, in a pathology lab, my enormous right ovary is sitting in a specimen bag, waiting to be tested.

'You should consider your fertility options as a matter

of some urgency,' the consultant says, and instead of refusing to respond and having an existential meltdown about what it would mean to have children, or not to have children, and how the absence of Max in my life changes all of that, and dragging poor Mrs Gaskell into it, too, I just nod and say, 'I will.'

Because in this version, I have made a decision to take what I can have from life despite what I cannot; to make the choices that are available to me; to be an author and not a critic. It is possible, I realize, to inhabit a world of half measures – of being in love and not in love, of having one ovary instead of two – and still do some things wholly. I understand that Mrs Gaskell and Charles Eliot Norton never so much as kissed, but that they were in love from the moment they met, until the days they died, thousands of miles and forty-three years apart. I understand that I will never marry Max and also that part of me will always wonder what would have happened if I did. I understand that I can't have him, but that what I can have, nonetheless, is a baby.

And so I'll return to the catalogue of sperm donors, and I'll drink wine with Izra and Holly and Louise and make a game of it at first, filtering the online database by hair colour, or religion, or height and seeing what comes up. Then I'll be serious, and imagine each of these generous, anonymous men as the father of my child, and I'll imagine the child too: a beloved stranger. Soon after that, I'll make a choice. I'll fill out the paperwork. I'll begin.

This is not an ending in the way that Mrs Gaskell has an ending in this book. I do not die. Instead, I have reached a brief moment of clarity, and I have grasped hold of it. I have made a choice. Nothing is really over, but maybe the idea that things will ever be over is over.

In all these scenarios, though, it is only fair that Mrs Gaskell gets a rewrite too. In these endings, Mrs Gaskell gets to go to America.

The End: Mrs Gaskell
Goes to America

You couldn't breathe easily until you had reached the open water. In your dreams you never made it that far, always floundering in the Liverpool docks before you found the ocean, always waking up before you truly set off. But the steamer was coasting through the waves, now, and if you stood on deck you could feel the air changing, the salt-laced wind, the clear, unfiltered quality of the light far out to sea.

You were going to America.

The journey reminded you, of course, of your voyage to Rome all those years ago, the succession of sunrises and sunsets, the patterns of colours playing on the water at night, the early morning stillness. You had been with your girls, then, and hadn't known, as you did this time, that Mr Norton was waiting on the other side. As you set off from Marseille, gliding past the Château d'If, you had not known that your life was about to change.

This time around, you were alone. Your girls had all grown up. You were a solo voyager to the New World, and you were going to see your old, dear friend, with whom you were – had always been – in love.

For the thousandth time, you tried to imagine America. You recalled the photographs you had seen of its houses and cities, the stories you'd read of its forests. You took out Mr Norton's letters and read the descriptions of his home in Boston, his garden, his study, words and images that had made you ache with longing when you had first read them, and made you ache still. You were going to see them with your own eyes.

The wind grasped the last page of an old letter from your hand and blew it out of reach, above the deck and then out, over the ocean. You watched it flap and flutter above the water, then get caught in a wave and sucked under.

The letters you had sent, one after another, across the Atlantic to Mr Norton, would all be waiting for you in his house in Massachusetts. The words you wrote were no longer replacements for you, only precursors.

Day after day, night after night, your ship crept around the curve of the globe. Above you the clouds and sun and moon shifted around each other in the sky. Beneath you were the carcasses of ships and people who had sailed before you and failed to stay afloat. Somewhere down there was the page of Mr Norton's letter that had fluttered away from you into the water. Somewhere was the skeleton of Margaret Fuller, the American journalist who had lived in Rome and drowned in 1850 with her husband and baby. Nearby would be the vast statue of John Calhoun that Hiram Powers had tried to send to America on the same ship, and which had gone down along with every other passenger on board. There were countless lives and stories down there on the ocean bed. Swathed in seaweed, John Calhoun's marble face was staring up at you.

You kept your mind on the surface of the water, and on the world ahead. The first sign of land on the horizon was, the captain said, Newfoundland, and even the name of it made your heart sing. The ship moved south. Nova Scotia. Maine. Small green islands pushed up through the water near the coast, more vibrant and solid, you thought, than any English version you had ever seen. The Old World had nothing at all on this bright new continent where, one morning, after two weeks at sea, a cry on deck summoned you up to look out at a broad new city, a harbour flecked with white-sailed boats, and a crowd of people waiting on the shore to greet the ship.

New York, the passengers around you murmured, and you said it to yourself: 'New York.' New life, new chapter, new opportunity, new world. New York.

There was a crush of porters and hustlers and tradesmen and newspaper-sellers as you disembarked the ship, and shouting all around, and you craned your neck to look over the heads of the rabble, searching for that one familiar face, which you had sailed for weeks to find. And then, at last, there it was. He was there, waiting for you with a bunch of violets in one hand, as though no time at all had passed since your breakfasts at Casa Cabrale, as though nothing had changed.

His face amongst the others in the crowd was hopeful, smiling, sunlit, looking just as you first saw it.

Newport Community
Learning & Libraries

Thanks—

To Rebecca Carter, my agent at Janklow & Nesbit,
    for telling me to write this book when it was just
    a passing thought; for her ability to turn big
    problems into small ones, and small ones into
    thin air; for friendship.
To Sophie Jonathan, who is sharp and generous, who
    finds in my words the story they were meant to be,
    and without whom I'd never get outed on Upper
    Street.
To Kris Puopolo for perfectly worded advice, infectious
    zeal, seeing the best in my writing and being
    infinitely tactful about the worst.
To Lynn Henry for support, enthusiasm and good ideas.
To Emma Parry at Janklow & Nesbit in New York, whose
    brilliance is always palpable from this side of the
    Atlantic.
To the many people at Picador in the UK, Doubleday
    in the US, and Knopf in Canada, including Gillian
    Fitzgerald-Kelly, Justine Anweiler, Daniel Meyer and
    many others, who have transformed fragmented
    word documents on my laptop into books you can
    hold.
To Leslie Epstein for a lifetime's worth of lessons.

To my Ph.D. supervisor at King's College London, the
staff at the Harry Ransom Center at the University
of Texas, and the Arts and Humanities Research
Council, for supporting me during the strange years
of my Ph.D.

To Gabrielle Mearns for hospital visits, night-time phone
calls and Italian days.

To Amanda Walker, Claudia Gray and Grace Shortland,
for helping me out from under the coffee table.

To Laura Marris for steadfastness, margaritas, clarity and
poetry.

To Nick Stone for bagels on the Highline and a summer
in New York.

To Lena Dunham for support and solidarity.

To Margaret and Richard for continuing to parent me
long after any of us could have imagined it would
be necessary.

To Simon and Emily for thinking about things so clearly
and so wisely.

To the man who is like and not like Max in this story, for
his generosity, integrity, graciousness and courage.

To Eley Williams, plot twist & plot twister.

And, finally, to you, Mrs Gaskell, my great friend.

Newport Library and
Information Service

21.6.19